REFERENCE GUIDES IN LITERATURE

NUMBER 8

Ronald Gottesman, *Editor*
Joseph Katz, *Consulting Editor*

John Berryman: A Reference Guide

Gary Q. Arpin

G. K. HALL & CO., 70 LINCOLN STREET, BOSTON, MASS.

Library of Congress Cataloging in Publication Data

Arpin, Gary Q
    John Berryman.

    (Reference guides in literature ; no. 8)
    Includes index.
    1.   Berryman, John, 1914-1972--Bibliography.
Z8091.43.A76 [PS3503.E744] 016.811'5'4   76-2491
ISBN 0-8161-7804-6

This publication is printed on permanent/durable acid free paper
MANUFACTURED IN THE UNITED STATES OF AMERICA

Contents

Introduction

John Berryman's career may be divided into three periods. In the first period, culminating with the publication, in 1948, of The Dispossessed, Berryman sought a style of his own, a language equal to his sensibility. The poetry of this period is heavily influenced, most frequently by Yeats and Auden, Berryman's early masters. The work of Berryman's major period--Homage to Mistress Bradstreet and The Dream Songs--is the result of his having found his own style, one that is idiosyncratic and powerful, marked especially by distortions of syntax and the juxtaposition of formal, archaic and colloquial diction. Before he died in 1972, Berryman had written two books of poetry in a new style, disarmingly simple and frankly, although at times ambiguously, devotional. He spoke in interviews given in the years before his death of the simplicity and "transparency" of high art. His work was clearly moving in a new direction.

Criticism of Berryman's work may also be divided into three periods, although they do not strictly parallel the periods of his career. His early work achieved recognition chiefly among intellectuals and fellow-poets. Reviews of his work appeared with regularity only in a handful of influential periodicals. With the publication of Homage to Mistress Bradstreet in 1956, however, his reputation began to spread, and by 1964, when 77 Dream Songs was published, his work was receiving a great deal of attention from the popular press. Finally, by the time of his death, Berryman's poetry was beginning to be the subject of serious and widespread scholarly examination.

INTRODUCTION

The criticism in each of these periods has its advantages and its drawbacks. The most consistently intelligent criticism was written in the first period. It could hardly have been otherwise, since it was written by some of the most sensitive and intelligent men in American letters—Allen Tate, Randall Jarrell and John Crowe Ransom, among others. However, comparatively little was written during this period; Berryman's achievement at this point, after all, was fairly modest. A great deal more was written about Berryman during the period of his widest recognition, from the mid-1950's until his death. More was written, but it was less consistently good. Frequently, as in the earlier criticism, the most perceptive and informed work was written by Berryman's fellow-poets—Adrienne Rich, William Meredith and Robert Fitzgerald come to mind immediately. In recent years, Berryman's work has been receiving the attention of scholars and literary critics, and it will doubtless continue to do so for many years hence. A thorough scholarly examination of Berryman's work should help us all better understand and appreciate his achievement.

It is the purpose of this bibliography to assist students and scholars interested in Berryman's work. Each listing is accompanied by an abstract which is intended to aid the reader in determining whether the item will be of use or not. The abstract is obviously not intended to be a substitute for the item, nor is it intended to be a judgement of it. No bibliography is complete. I have tried, however, to make this one complete through 1974, with the following exceptions: references to Berryman's critical work on Stephen Crane in books and articles about Crane have been omitted (I have, of course, included reviews of Stephen Crane, but to include more would, I felt, carry the bibliography too far afield); nonsubstantial references to Berryman in literary histories and the like have been omitted; with a very few exceptions, introductions to Berryman's work in anthologies of poetry have been omitted; Who's Who and other standard directory entries have been omitted. I have not included poems about Berryman, nor, with one

INTRODUCTION

exception, have I included Berryman's own work.   The 1975
listings must be considered partial.

No bibliography is complete, but this one would have
been a great deal less complete if it had not been for
the assistance of many people.   Richard Kelly's <u>John
Berryman: A Checklist</u> proved to be an admirable starting
point for this work, as did Ernest Stefanik's bibliogra-
phical work on Berryman.   I was further assisted by the
running bibliographies in <u>John Berryman Studies</u> prepared
by Mr. Kelly and Professor Stefanik.   Mr. Kelly very
kindly provided me with photocopies of material I was
having difficulty procuring.   Professor Stefanik checked
references for me and also provided copies of hard-to-
find items; his willingness and ability to help me were
virtually boundless, and for this I am deeply grateful.
Professor Toshikazu Niikura of Meiji Gakuin University,
Tokyo, very kindly prepared abstracts of some material
written in Japanese, and also supplied references to
items I had been unaware of.   Mr. David Campbell provided me a great deal of help in running down difficult
references.   I am, of course, responsible for all errors
in this book.

I would like to thank the staff of the Western Illinois University Memorial Library for their assistance,
especially Mrs. Elosia Mitchell, who spent a great deal
of time and energy obtaining material for me.   I am also
indebted to my colleagues in the Department of English
at Western Illinois University, especially its chairman,
Professor Robert Jacobs, for allowing me to take time
from my other duties to complete this work.

I could not have completed this book without the
assistance of my wife, Susan, who helped in translating,
indexing and in dozens of other smaller, but no less
important ways.

Abbreviations

The following abbreviations are used
in this book.

AQ	American Quarterly
AR	Antioch Review
ASch	American Scholar
BB	Bulletin of Bibliography
CentR	Centennial Review (Michigan State University)
ChiR	Chicago Review
ConL	Contemporary Literature
CP	Concerning Poetry
CritQ	Critical Quarterly
EA	Etudes Anglaises
EigoS	Eigo Seinen [The Rising Generation] (Tokyo)
Expl	Explicator
GaR	Georgia Review
HudR	Hudson Review
JML	Journal of Modern Literature
KR	Kenyon Review
LJ	Library Journal
MinnR	Minnesota Review
MR	Massachusetts Review
NCF	Nineteenth-Century Fiction
NEQ	New England Quarterly
NLH	New Literary History (University of Virginia)
NY	New Yorker
OhR	Ohio Review

ABBREVIATIONS

PoetryR	Poetry Review (London)
PR	Partisan Review
PrS	Prairie Schooner
RES	Review of English Studies
SAQ	South Atlantic Quarterly
SatR	Saturday Review
SHR	Southern Humanities Review
SoR	Southern Review (Louisiana State University)
SoRA	Southern Review: An Australian Journal of Literary Studies (University of Adelaide)
SR	Sewanee Review
SRL	Saturday Review of Literature
SWR	Southwest Review
TLS	Times Literary Supplement (London)
TSLL	Texas Studies in Literature and Language
UWR	University of Windsor Review (Windsor, Ontario)
VQR	Virginia Quarterly Review
WCR	West Coast Review
WR	Western Review: A Journal of the Humanities
WSCL	Wisconsin Studies in Contemporary Literature
YR	Yale Review

Writings About John Berryman, 1935 - 1975

1935 A BOOKS - NONE

1935 B SHORTER WRITINGS

   1   ANON. "Oklahoma Man Wins Columbia Verse Prize,"
New York Times (22 December), p. 10B.
Notice of Berryman's winning the Van
Rensselaer prize for "Note on E. A. Robinson."

1937 A BOOKS - NONE

1937 B SHORTER WRITINGS

   1   ANON. "Wins Cambridge Honor," New York Times
(12 December), p. 5B.
Notice of Berryman's receiving the Oldham
Shakespeare Fellowship at Cambridge. Pic-
ture.

1939 A BOOKS - NONE

1939 B SHORTER WRITINGS

   1   STEDMAN, JANE. "Poet, Editor, Teacher--Looks
Forward to Own Book," The Detroit Collegian
[Wayne University] (23 October), p. 2.

1939

(STEDMAN, JANE)
Primarily a description of Berryman's
methods of soliciting and printing poems in
his capacity as poetry editor of the Nation.

1940 A BOOKS - NONE

1940 B SHORTER WRITINGS

1   HOLMES, JOHN. "Poems and Things," Boston Eve-
         ning Transcript (16 December), p. 9.
            Review of Five Young American Poets. The
         verse of all of the poets in this volume is
         stiff and intellectual, but promising.
         Berryman is one of the best in the volume.

1941 A BOOKS - NONE

1941 B SHORTER WRITINGS

1   ANON. "Verse," NY, XVI (18 January), 80.
            Brief notice describing Five Young American
         Poets.

2   AIKEN, CONRAD. "Poetry: What Direction?" New
         Republic, CIV (12 May), 670-71.
            Review of Five Young American Poets. The
         poets in this volume are too self-conscious.
         Despite some good pieces by Berryman and
         others, the work is diluted with "vin
         Audenaire."

3   BLACKMUR, R. P. "Twelve Poets," SoR, VII (Sum-
         mer), 187-213.
            Review of Five Young American Poets and
         other volumes. Berryman is the "maturest

(BLACKMUR, R. P.)
and ablest" of the five, and although his work
is heavily influenced, some of his poems come
close to establishing their own forms.

4   CONRAD, SHERMAN. "The New Intellectualism: Two
Views. II: Poetry as a Jackdaw's Nest,"
Poetry, LVIII (May), 90-96.
Reply to Scott (1941.B10). Discussion of
recent tendencies in poetry using _Five Young_
American Poets and one other volume as texts.
Recent poets' attention to technique is di-
rected towards expression of emotion. These
poets have new knowledge of the language of
poetry and are using that knowledge effec-
tively.

5   DANIEL, ROBERT. "A Glimpse of the Future," _SR_,
XLIX (October-December), 553-61.
Review of _Five Young American Poets_.
Berryman is at his best when dealing indi-
rectly with his principal theme, the troubled
modern world. One of the "promises" of his
style is the ability to use "the ordinary
elements of city life" in his work.

6   DEUTSCH, BABETTE. "The Younger Generation," New
York _Herald Tribune Books_ (12 January), p. 13.
Review of _Five Young American Poets_. Men-
tions that some of Berryman's poems are
"memorable," but the volume contains no po-
tentially great talent.

7   FRANKENBERG, LLOYD. "Five Directions," _Nation_,
CLIII (19 July), 56-57.
Review of _Five Young American Poets_.
Berryman's prose note to his selection tends
to "reduce poetry to solvable cryptograms,"
a tendency exemplified by some of his verse.

3

1941

8   MILES, JOSEPHINE. "Nothing for Granted," Accent,
        1 (Spring), 185-86.
            Review of Five Young American Poets. These
        poets are representative of the modern tra-
        dition, abstract, difficult, "taking nothing
        for granted." They allow themselves no "sur-
        face satisfaction;" they should relax their
        verse a bit.

9   RANSOM, JOHN CROWE. "Constellation of Five Young
        Poets," KR, III (Summer), 377-80.
            Review of Five Young American Poets. Brief
        mention of Berryman as one of the most pro-
        ficient of the five, although Randall Jarrell
        is described as "the most brilliant."

10   SCOTT, W[INFIELD] T[OWNLEY]. "The New Intellec-
        tualism: Two Views. I. The Dry Reaction,"
        Poetry, LVIII (May), 86-90.
            Discussion of recent tendencies in poetry
        using Five Young American Poets and one other
        volume as texts. Notes the increasing "dry-
        ness" of recent poetry, the emphasis on tech-
        nique and intelligence rather than emotion.
        Berryman is the "most skilled" of the group,
        but what one notices about his verse is "the
        method." See also 1941.B4.

11   TATE, ALLEN. "The Last Omnibus," PR, VIII (May-
        June), 241-44 [243-44].
            Review of Five Young American Poets and
        other volumes. Berryman and Randall Jarrell
        are the best of the five, but they are over-
        influenced. Yeats is too noticeable in and
        constraining to Berryman's work.

12   W[ILLIAMS], O[SCAR]. Review of Five Young Ameri-
        can Poets. Living Age, CCCLIX (January),
        496-98.

4

(W[ILLIAMS], O[SCAR])
      Berryman is the best poet in the volume,
Randall Jarrell is the worst. Berryman's
ear, style and "compassion" are praise-
worthy.

1942 A BOOKS - NONE

1942 B SHORTER WRITINGS

  1   FRYE, NORTHRUP. "Books of the Month: Poetry,"
          Canadian Forum, XXII (October), 220.
          Review of Berryman's Poems and one other
      volume. Bemoans the fact that so many poets
      are writing only about Fascism and the war.
      This new "convention of the elegiac lament
      over contemporary evils" is boring, and al-
      though some of Berryman's poems are powerful,
      his work is really just another contribution
      to this convention.

  2   JARRELL, RANDALL. "In All Directions," PR, IX
          (July), 345-47 [347].
          Review of New Directions, 1941. Brief
      description of Berryman's "Five Political
      Poems": "lots of Yeats, lots of general
      politics."

  3   STRACHAN, PEARL. "The World of Poetry," Chris-
          tian Science Monitor (3 October), p. 10.
          Review of Berryman's Poems and other works.
      Berryman's poetry stirs up the "right kind
      of protest" against social ills. His verse
      has "a genuine poetic quality."

1943

1943 A   BOOKS - NONE

1943 B   SHORTER WRITINGS

    1   DEUTSCH, BABETTE. "Poets--Timely and Timeless,"
        New Republic, CVIII (29 March), 420-21.
          Review of Poems and ten other volumes in
        the "Poet of the Month" Series. Berryman's
        poetry is not particularly distinguished.
        His work is over-influenced, and repetitions
        in the style (like "Admit, admit") are
        annoying.

    2   JONES, FRANK. "Skilled Workers," Nation, CLVI
        (17 April), 569-70.
          Review of Berryman's Poems and other works.
        Berryman's work is generally "very young,
        very taut, very solemn," and heavily in-
        fluenced by Yeats. He is at his best when
        his tone is more relaxed, as in "Communist"
        and "A Poem for Bhain," which are indications
        of better work to come.

1946 A   BOOKS - NONE

1946 B   SHORTER WRITINGS

    1   GREG, W. W. "Correspondence: The Staging of
        King Lear," RES, XXII (July), 229.
          Greg writes to say that an "exchange of
        views" with Berryman has led Greg to change
        his ideas about the staging of Lear.

1948 A   BOOKS - NONE

1948 B   SHORTER WRITINGS

1948

1 ANON. Review of The Dispossessed, Kirkus Reviews,
       XVI (1 April), 185.
          Berryman is an "accomplished craftsman"
       whose work is heavily influenced by the work
       of Wallace Stevens, although his ideas are
       not as important as those of Stevens.

2 ANON. "An American Poet," TLS, XLVII (3 July),
       374.
          Review of The Dispossessed. The more rig-
       orous criticism of poetry in America has made
       for more craftsmanlike and disciplined poems,
       of which Berryman's verse is an example.
       Even Berryman's poems in the manner of Yeats
       result in more than pastiche.

3 ANON. "Verse," NY, XXIV (2 October), 107-08.
          Brief review of The Dispossessed, noting
       that Berryman has mastered the rhetoric of
       modern verse, but has no "fire and sting."

4 ANON. "News Notes," Poetry, LXXIII (November),
       104.
          Notice of Berryman's winning the Guarantors'
       Prize of $100 for "Five Poems."

5 BARKER, SHIRLEY. Review of The Dispossessed, LJ,
       LXXIII (15 July), 948.
          Brief review of these "intelligent, honest"
       poems.

6 DAICHES, DAVID. "Wit, Sense and Poetry," New
       York Herald Tribune Book Review (21 November),
       p. 22.
          Review of The Dispossessed and one other
       volume. Notes the quiet, period style of the
       early poems. When Berryman tries to be more
       passionate, as in "Canto Amor," he fails.

1948

7   EBERHART, RICHARD. "Song of the Nerves," Poetry,
        LXXIII (October), 43-45.
            Review of The Dispossessed, praising Berry-
        man's technical abilities--especially his use
        of language--and the "peculiarity of his mind."

8   FERRIL, THOMAS. "Some Recent Poetry," San Fran-
        cisco Chronicle (5 December), p. 19.
            Review of The Dispossessed and other works.
        Berryman's poetry presents "something wistful"
        hidden behind a "sophisticated mask," as if
        there were a conflict between what Berryman
        wanted to say and his desire to write
        "aesthetically approved poetry."

9   FIEDLER, LESLIE. "Some Uses and Failures of
        Feeling," PR, XV (August), 924-31 [926-27].
            Review of The Dispossessed and other volumes.
        Berryman, like the other poets under review,
        is attempting to extend the range of expres-
        sion in his verse. He does this successfully
        in poems like "Canto Amor," although there is
        a "problem of expression" in some of his other
        poems.

10 FITTS, DUDLEY. "Deep in the Unfriendly City,"
        New York Times Book Review (20 June), p. 4.
            Review of The Dispossessed. There is a fine
        skill exhibited in these poems, but "a certain
        sense of muzziness" keeps them from succeeding
        as often as they should. Berryman is at his
        best when he is least pretentious, when he
        avoids the "deep in the unfriendly city" tone.

11 FITZGERALD, ROBERT. "Poetry and Perfection," SR,
        LVI (August), 685-97 [690-93].
            Review of The Dispossessed and other vol-
        umes. Praises Berryman's technical abilities,

1948

(FITZGERALD, ROBERT)
    analyzing, as an example of those abilities,
    "The Disciple," but notes that Berryman's
    verse is too studied and literary.

12 JARRELL, RANDALL. "Verse Chronicle," Nation,
    CLXVII (17 July), 80-81.
        Review of The Dispossessed and other works.
    Berryman's poetry "has steadily improved."
    His early work was too heavily influenced, but
    his new, very individualistic style, first
    seen in "The Nervous Songs," fits Berryman's
    "knowledge and sensibility surprisingly well."
    Although the style overwhelms the subject
    matter in these poems, we can look forward
    "with real curiosity and pleasure" to Berry-
    man's future work.

13 KENNEDY, LEO. "Special Month for Poetry," Chica-
    go Sun-Times (31 May), p. 46.
        Berryman's concern, in The Dispossessed,
    for the problems of modern life makes his
    work especially relevant in 1948. Berryman's
    "vision is of a world whirling its way to an
    atomized Hell."

14 MERTON, THOMAS. The Seven-Storey Mountain. New
    York: Harcourt, Brace & Co., p. 155.
        Brief description of Berryman at Columbia,
    the "star" of the literary magazine and "the
    most earnest-looking man on campus."

15 MEYER, GERARD PREVIN. "Vigorous Swimmer in the
    Poetic Stream," SRL, XXXI (10 July), 21.
        Review of The Dispossessed. Praises Berry-
    man's sense of form, and notes that although
    he is a "'learned'" poet, he writes out of
    his and our experience.

1948

16   NIMS, JOHN FREDERICK. Comment on "The Dispos-
         sessed," "World's Fair," and "The Traveler,"
         Poetry: A Critical Supplement (April), 1-6.
            Comment addressed principally to under-
         graduate students, but the discussion of
         "The Dispossessed" is fairly long and sub-
         stantial in spite of the fact that it does
         not mention the atomic bomb.

17   SWALLOW, ALAN. "Some Current Poetry," New Mexico
         Quarterly Review, XVIII (Winter), 455-62.
            Review of The Dispossessed and eighteen
         other works. Compares Berryman's work with
         Henry Reed's--their poetry represents a "re-
         action to Eliot, Yeats and Auden as gods of
         the young poet." Berryman's work is more
         confused and less original than Reed's, and
         he is best at poems that utilize a "ruminative
         rhetoric."

18   WEISS, NEIL. "The Grace and the Hysteria," New
         Leader, XXXI (3 July), 10.
            Review of The Dispossessed and Mark Van
         Doren's New Poems. The "grace" is Van Doren's,
         the "hysteria" is Berryman's. Berryman's
         "powerful deformation of language" is appro-
         priate to our time. In technique and style,
         he can be favorably compared with the best of
         the young poets.

19   WINTERS, YVOR. "Three Poets," HudR, I (Autumn),
         404-05.
            Review of The Dispossessed and other vol-
         umes. Finds some indication in Berryman's
         verse of a talent for language, but most of
         the poems are only partially-realized varia-
         tions of the theme of modern chaos. Berryman
         has to "learn to think more and feel less."

1950

(WINTERS, YVOR)
Reprinted in Yvor Winters: Uncollected
Essays and Reviews, edited by Francis Murphy.
Chicago: Swallow Press, 1973, 167-73
[1975.B85].

1949 A BOOKS - NONE

1949 B SHORTER WRITINGS

1 GRIFFIN, HOWARD. "The Cold Heart, The Cold City,"
    Voices, CXXXVI (Winter), 52-54.
       Review of The Dispossessed and other vol-
    umes. Berryman is "only vaguely" disturbed
    by human evil. The scope of his poems is not
    wide; it would be broadened if he wouldn't
    concentrate, as he does increasingly in his
    more recent poems, on the "creation of in-
    tricate verbality." Berryman should return
    to the style of earlier poems like "White
    Feather."

1950 A BOOKS - NONE

1950 B SHORTER WRITINGS

1 ANON. "Poet Wins Fellowship," New York Times
    (20 March), p. 19.
       Notice of Berryman's winning the Alfred
    Hodder Fellowship at Princeton for 1950-51.

2 ANON. Review of Stephen Crane, Kirkus Reviews,
    XVIII (15 August), 496.
       Berryman's psychoanalytical biography of
    Crane overlays Crane's life with "a patina
    of Kafka." The book is harmed by its humor-
    lessness, its "affected style" and a "Partisan

11

1950

(ANON.)
> Review" orientation, but is nonetheless an important contribution to literary scholarship.

3   ANON. "News Notes," Poetry, LXXVII (November), 85.
> Notice of the award of the Levinson Prize of $100 to Berryman for "Eight Poems."

4   ANON. "Man in Search of a Hero," Time, LVI (25 December), 58-59.
> Review of Stephen Crane, describing Crane's career. Berryman's study is mentioned only briefly.

5   DAVIS, ROBERT GORHAM. "The Fascinating Mr. Stephen Crane," New York Times Book Review (10 December), pp. 4, 18.
> Review of Stephen Crane. Berryman's style obtrudes in this otherwise useful book. Berryman's use of Freud makes even the critical parts of the book "largely biographical."

6   HART, H. W. Review of Stephen Crane, LJ, LXXV (1 September), 1396.
> Brief review, calling Berryman's psychoanalytic interpretations "ambitious."

7   JACKSON, JOSEPH HENRY. "Bookman's Notebook: Our First 'Modern' Writer," San Francisco Chronicle (20 December), p. 18.
> Berryman's biography manages to cover Crane's life very thoroughly in a limited space, but its real excellence lies in the picture Berryman draws of Crane's mind and work. His analysis—which transcends the Freudian hodge-podge of other recent critical biographies—makes the book indispensable for all students of Crane.

8   PRESCOTT, ORVILLE. "Books of the Times," New
         York Times (12 December), p. 31.
            Review of Stephen Crane. The book is more
         complete and accurate than Thomas Beer's
         biography, but the style is "wretchedly bad"
         and the Freudian analysis is "pretentious."
         Berryman's literary judgement makes for "a
         strange book."

9   STILLMAN, CLARA GRUENING. "Stephen Crane, That
         Long Neglected Genius of Imaginative Realism,"
         New York Herald Tribune Book Review (17
         December), p. 5.
            Review of Stephen Crane, noting especially
         the ambitious Freudian analysis, which is
         "strikingly original."

1951 A   BOOKS - NONE

1951 B   SHORTER WRITINGS

1   ANON. Review of Stephen Crane, Booklist, XLVII
         (15 January), 187.
            The biography is usually perceptive, de-
         spite the "glib" use of Freudian psychology,
         which is not completely convincing.

2   ANON. Review of Stephen Crane, U.S. Quarterly
         Book Review, VII (June), 140.
            Berryman's style and the Freudian interpre-
         tations in the last chapter mar what is other-
         wise a fine piece of work.

3   ANON. "Badge of Courage," TLS, L (8 June), 356.
            Review of Stephen Crane which describes
         Crane's career and critical reception, men-
         tioning Berryman's study only near the end
         with a disdainful remark about its Freudianism.

1951

4   ANON. Review of <u>Stephen Crane</u>, <u>The Listener</u>
      (19 July), 112-13.
       Although it was necessary to include
      Stephen Crane in the American Men of Letters
      series, the job Berryman has done is weak
      compared with the other volumes in that series.
      Berryman spends too much time summarizing the
      stories, the final chapter is jargon-ridden,
      and the style is "often ugly."

5   ANON. "Princeton Poet Named to Cincinnati U.
      Chair," <u>New York Times</u> (5 December), p. 17.
       Notice of Berryman's being named to the
      George Elliston Poetry Chair at the University
      of Cincinnati for the second semester of 1951.

6   AARON, DANIEL. "Stephen Crane," <u>HudR</u>, IV
      (Autumn), 471-73.
       Review of <u>Stephen Crane</u>. Much of the bio-
      graphical material is simply a repetition of
      Thomas Beer's work, although Berryman brings
      Beer up to date. The most valuable parts of
      the book are the discussions of Crane's art
      in the last two chapters.

7   ABERCROMBIE, RALPH. "American Story-Teller,"
      <u>Spectator</u>, CLXXXVI (29 June), 870.
       Review of <u>Stephen Crane</u>. Berryman's ground-
      breaking work should make English readers
      aware of Crane's achievements.

8   BEACH, JOSEPH WARREN. "Five Makers of American
      Fiction," <u>YR</u>, XL (Summer), 744-51 [744-47].
       Review of <u>Stephen Crane</u> and other books.
      Berryman is at his best when discussing
      Crane's irony and applying Freudian insights
      to the life and work; the most notable lapse
      is the lack of attention paid to Crane's early
      style.

1951

9   BLUM, MORGAN. "Berryman as Biographer, Stephen
         Crane as Poet," Poetry, LXXVIII (August),
         298-307.
             Review of Stephen Crane. Berryman's biog-
         raphy is "flawed and distinguished"--flawed
         by the lack of documentation and lack of com-
         prehensive criticism, distinguished in its
         insights into the way writers act and in its
         treatment of the relations between Crane's
         life and his work.

10   BOOCHEVER, FLORENCE. Review of Stephen Crane,
         Bookmark, X (January), 81.
             Berryman's work is a "discerning critical
         study" which offers a new appraisal of Crane
         and his work.

11   BURFORD, WILLIAM. "Majesty and Trash," SWR,
         XXXVI (Summer), xii-xv.
             Review of Stephen Crane. The "majesty" of
         Berryman's book is the literary criticism,
         which is first-rate; the "trash" is the
         application of depth-psychology to Crane's
         life. Berryman's discussion of Crane as an
         'impressionist' is good, but Berryman should
         have chosen a more appropriate term, such as
         'expressionist.'

12   CLARKE, CLORINDA. Review of Stephen Crane,
         Catholic World, CLXXIII (May), 158-59.
             Berryman's style and his reliance on Freud
         are "definite handicaps," but the biography
         and critical analyses are useful.

13   COURNOS, JOHN. Review of Stephen Crane, Common-
         weal, LIII (12 January), 356-57.
             The book is faulted by its reliance on
         psychoanalytical ideas, but the discussion of
         Crane the creative artist "is singularly
         penetrating."

15

1951

14   GREENE, GRAHAM. "The Badge of Courage," <u>New
     Statesman and Nation</u>, XLI (2 June), 627-28.
         Review of <u>Stephen Crane</u>. Berryman's
     "tortured prose," weak critical judgements
     and use of "pseudo-Freudian" ideas make the
     work unsatisfactory.

15   HAVIGHURST, WALTER. "Book Accurately Surveys
     Stephen Crane's Career," Chicago <u>Sunday
     Tribune Book Week</u> (4 February), p. 5.
         Brief review of <u>Stephen Crane</u>, noting that
     the book is "accurate and penetrating."

16   HOLLIS, C. CARROLL. "Stephen Crane," <u>America</u>,
     LXXXIV (17 February), 591.
         <u>Stephen Crane</u> is a well-written and sensi-
     tive biography; its only drawback is its re-
     liance on Freudian notions of creativity.

17   JONES, CLAUDE. "Stephen Crane," <u>NCF</u>, VI (June),
     74-76.
         The biographical presentation in <u>Stephen
     Crane</u> is successful, as is Berryman's treat-
     ment of Crane's art, but the Freudian inter-
     pretations of the last chapter are "semi-
     scientific gobbledegook."

18   MARKFIELD, WALLACE. "Stephen Crane: Cynic and
     Cavalier," <u>New Leader</u>, XXXIV (15 January),
     21-22.
         Berryman's biography of Crane is marked by
     a sensitivity to aspects of Crane's work
     previously unnoticed--his divergence from
     Naturalism and his faith in the human will.
     A kinship between Berryman as a critic and
     his subject enables us to more fully under-
     stand Crane as a despairing American artist
     who "must mutilate his life and talents."

1951

19   MITCHELL, DANIEL T.   "Critical Biography of
        Stephen Crane," Books on Trial, IX (February),
        234-35.
            The main difficulty in Berryman's biography
        is caused by the limitations imposed on it by
        the American Men of Letters series. Berryman
        doesn't have the room to develop his arguments
        completely, and so they are only partially
        convincing.

20   MONAS, SIDNEY.   "Stephen Crane, Impressionist,"
        Hopkins Review, IV (Spring), 57-59.
            The psychoanalytic insights in Berryman's
        biography explain much in Crane's work.
        Berryman's style calls attention to itself
        in its "tortured syntax." The book is dif-
        ficult and occasionally arrogant, but the
        reader will learn a great deal from it about
        Crane and "something about excellent biography."

21   SPILLER, ROBERT E.   "Great Stylist," SRL (27 Jan-
        uary), 11.
            Berryman's biography of Stephen Crane does
        not add greatly to our knowledge of Crane's
        life, but his discussions of Crane's "art and
        soul" are impressive.

22   STONE, EDWARD.   Review of Stephen Crane, SAQ, L
        (July), 440-41.
            Berryman's Freudian analysis lacks the hard
        evidence to make it fully convincing; never-
        theless, both as biography and criticism the
        book is eminently successful.

23   WANNING, ANDREWS.   "A Portrait of Stephen Crane,"
        PR, XVIII (May-June), 358-61.
            Berryman's biography of Crane is strongest
        in its discussion of Crane's art. The

1951

(WANNING, ANDREWS)
Freudian insights into Crane's life and work,
however, seem to be based on thin evidence.

24 WILSON, EDMUND. "Stephen Crane--Hannah Whitall
Smith," NY, XXVI (6 January), 77-85 [77-82].
Berryman's Stephen Crane is an important,
insightful book, especially good in its discussions of Crane's art. Although one cannot
be sure of Berryman's Freudian interpreta-
tions, they cannot be dismissed out of hand.

25 ZABEL, MORTON D. "Hero and Victim," Nation,
CLXXII (24 February), 187-88.
Berryman's Stephen Crane is sympathetic
and perhaps over-enthusiastic in its estima-
tion of Crane's genius, but it is a successful discussion of Crane's life, and a "sig-
nificant study in the morality of contemporary art."

1952 A BOOKS - NONE

1952 B SHORTER WRITINGS

1 ANON. "News Notes," Poetry, LXXX (July), 246.
Notice of Berryman's receipt of a Guggenheim Fellowship for 1952-53.

2 FLANAGAN, JOHN T. Review of Stephen Crane, AL,
XXIII (January), 510-11.
Berryman is at his best when discussing
Crane's personality and his art. The book
is "marred by gaps," though, and Berryman's
critical opinion of Crane's importance is
overinflated.

3   HICKS, GRANVILLE. "Three Men of Letters," <u>SR</u>,
        LX (Winter), 149-56 [153-56].
            Berryman's biography of Crane is useful in
        both biographical and critical areas and is
        marred chiefly by Berryman's overestimation
        of Crane's achievement.

4   HUGHES, RILEY. Review of <u>Stephen Crane</u>, <u>Thought</u>,
        XXVII (Summer), 307.
            The biographical aspects of the book are
        satisfactory, but Berryman leans too heavily
        on Freud, and the book is "impressionistic
        and strutting."

5   LeBRETON, M. Review of <u>Stephen Crane</u>, <u>EA</u>, V
        (Fevrier), 86.
            The most debatable aspect of this "well-
        informed" but largely biographical study is
        the Freudian analysis in the last chapter.

6   WEBER, BROM. "Two American Men of Letters," <u>WR</u>,
        XVI (Summer), 329-34.
            Review of <u>Stephen Crane</u> and one other book.
        Berryman's biography is "primary in the
        history and criticism of American letters,"
        although it does not devote enough attention
        to the relation between Crane the man and
        Crane the artist.

1955 A BOOKS - NONE

1955 B SHORTER WRITINGS

1. BRINNIN, JOHN MALCOLM. <u>Dylan Thomas in America</u>.
        Boston: Little, Brown, pp. 278, 293.
            Brief account of Berryman's presence in
        Dylan Thomas' room when Thomas died.

1955

2   KUNITZ, STANLEY J., ED. "Berryman, John,"
     Twentieth Century Authors: First Supplement.
     New York: H. W. Wilson, pp. 83–84.
        Brief entry describing Berryman's career
     and critical reception up to 1953.

1956 A BOOKS - NONE

1956 B SHORTER WRITINGS

1   ANON. Review of Homage to Mistress Bradstreet,
        Booklist, LIII (1 September), 16.
           Brief review, noting the emphasis in the
        poem on Bradstreet the woman rather than
        Bradstreet the poet.

2   HOLMES, JOHN. "Speaking in Verse," New York Times
        Book Review (30 September), p. 18.
           Review of Homage to Mistress Bradstreet.
        The poem requires "much re-reading," but is
        well worth it. The power of the language of
        this "landmark in American poetry" is
        especially to be praised.

3   McDONALD, GERALD D. Review of Homage to Mistress
        Bradstreet, LJ, LXXXI (1 December), 2862.
           Brief review, describing the poem as
        "highly acclaimed."

4   MADDOCKS, MELVIN. "A Probing of Attitude,"
        Christian Science Monitor (20 December),
        p. 11.
           Homage to Mistress Bradstreet is an exami-
        nation of "religious attitude and mood," but
        behind the moral questions in the poem, there
        is little sense of a woman leading her daily
        life.

5   PEDEN, WILLIAM. Review of <u>Homage to Mistress
     Bradstreet</u>, <u>New Mexico Quarterly</u>, XXVI
     (Autumn), 289-91.
          Describes the poem as a "difficult" but
     not "obscurantist" examination of both an
     individual woman in New England and "Woman"
     in the "World."

6   STRUDWICK, DOROTHY. "Homage to Mr. Berryman,"
     <u>Ivory Tower</u> [University of Minnesota],
     (5 November), pp. 6, 16.
          Brief description of Berryman's career and
     discussion of <u>Homage to Mistress Bradstreet</u>
     based on an interview with Berryman.

7   WHITE, ELIZABETH WADE. Review of <u>Homage to Mis-
     tress Bradstreet</u>, <u>NEQ</u>, XXIX (December),
     545-48.
          Description of the poem, noting especially
     the difficult but rewarding style of the
     piece, and pointing out some historical
     errors: Sylvester and Quarles were not Anne
     Bradstreet's favorite poets and Anne Hutchin-
     son was not her "'closest friend.'"

<u>1957 A   BOOKS - NONE</u>

<u>1957 B   SHORTER WRITINGS</u>

1   ANON. "News Notes," <u>Poetry</u>, XC (April), 59.
          Notice of Berryman's receipt of the <u>Partisan
     Review</u> Fellowship in Poetry for 1957.

2   ANON. "Books--Authors," <u>New York Times</u> (20 May),
     p. 23.
          Notice of Berryman's winning the Harriet
     Monroe Poetry Prize ($500.) at the University
     of Chicago.

JOHN BERRYMAN: A REFERENCE GUIDE

3   ANON. Review of <u>Homage to Mistress Bradstreet</u>,
      <u>Seventeenth-Century Newsletter</u>, XV (Summer),
      25.
         Brief note describing the poem.

4   ANON. "News Notes," <u>Poetry</u>, XC (July), 261.
         Notice of the performance of <u>The Way of the
      Cross</u> in Minneapolis (text by Paul Claudel,
      translated by Berryman).

5   BENNETT, JOSEPH. "Sawdust and Wine," <u>HudR</u>, X
      (Spring), 126-31 [127-29].
         <u>Homage to Mistress Bradstreet</u> is not a poem
      that attempts to be great; it is, rather, an
      important minor work, an "essay" in "archaism"
      and tone, and as such is completely success-
      ful.

6   BOGAN, LOUISE. "Verse," <u>NY</u>, XXXIII (2 March),
      111-12.
         Brief note on <u>Homage to Mistress Bradstreet</u>,
      noting the similarities in language to Hop-
      kins.

7   CIARDI, JOHN. "The Researched Mistress," <u>SatR</u>,
      XL (23 March), 36-37.
         Review of <u>Homage to Mistress Bradstreet</u>,
      noting especially the rhythmic strength of
      Berryman's line, but also the tendency of
      that line to obscure the narrative.

8   DORN, NORMAN K. "Amidst Smokey Jazz or 'Neath
      the Boughs, the Poets Create," San Francisco
      <u>Chronicle</u> (8 September), p. 29.
         Brief note on <u>Homage to Mistress Bradstreet</u>.

9   ECKMAN, FREDERICK. "Moody's Ode: The Collapse
      of the Heroic," <u>University of Texas Studies
      in English</u>, XXXVI (1957), 80-92.

(ECKMAN, FREDERICK)
A comparison of the themes and styles of
William Vaughn Moody's "Ode in Time of Hesi-
tation" and Berryman's "Boston Common." The
first laments the "absence of heroism," the
second flatly denies that heroism can again
exist. See also 1972.B20.

10 FLINT, R. W. "A Romantic on Early New England,"
New Republic, CXXXVI (27 May), 28.
Berryman's verse before Homage to Mistress
Bradstreet was weakened by "a lack of sub-
stance," but the choice of Anne Bradstreet
for the subject of this poem remedies that
problem. The work has a few faults, but can
be favorably compared with The Wreck of the
Deutschland and "the best of Lowell."

11 FRASER, G. S. "Modern Poetry: The American
Accent," PR, XXIV (Winter), 131-39 [137-38].
Review of Homage to Mistress Bradstreet and
other volumes. Berryman brings the period
and the woman alive. The poem has "strength
and body."

12 GORDON, AMBROSE, JR. Review of Homage to Mistress
Bradstreet, YR, XLVI (Winter), 298-300.
Summary of the poem, noting that its triumph is in the "curious diction" that the
poem employs.

13 KUNITZ, STANLEY. "No Middle Flight," Poetry, XC
(July), 244-49.
Homage to Mistress Bradstreet is ultimately
a failure because of Berryman's attempt to
inflate the commonplace and everyday, but it
is a failure that is "worth more than most
successes," and one which places Berryman
"among our most gifted poets."

1957

14   LANGLAND, JOSEPH. "A Contrast of Excellence,"
          Northwest Review, I (Spring), 56-60.
              Review of Homage to Mistress Bradstreet and
          one other volume. Describes the poem as a
          breakthrough and singles out the style for
          special praise.

15   MAGILL, FRANK, ED. "Homage to Mistress Brad-
          street," Masterplots Annual, 1957. New York:
          Salem Press, pp. 119-22.
              Discussion of Anne Bradstreet's life and
          work in comparison to Berryman's poem, a
          "product of powerful synthesis," which uses
          the past in a way not done before in American
          poetry.

16   SCOTT, WINFIELD TOWNLEY. "Mistress Bradstreet
          and the Long Poem," Poetry Broadside, I
          (Spring), 5, 13.
              Notes the relation between the lyric and
          the long poem in modern verse, and briefly
          discusses the style of Homage to Mistress
          Bradstreet.

17   UPDIKE, JOHN. "Notes," NY, XXXII (26 January),
          28-29.
              Parodistic treatment of the self-conscious
          notes to modern poems, including those to
          Homage to Mistress Bradstreet.

1958 A BOOKS - NONE

1958 B SHORTER WRITINGS

1   NIMS, JOHN FREDERICK. "Homage in Measure to Mr.
          Berryman," PrS, XXXII (Spring), 1-7.
              Comprehensive review, describing the poem
          as a "gallant failure," noting the successful
          aspects (especially the linguistic effects),

(NIMS, JOHN FREDERICK)
the less successful aspects (the historical
falsifications in service of Berryman's own
puritanism), and the theme (the poet's personality).

2   VAN DOREN, MARK. <u>The Autobiography of Mark Van
Doren</u>. New York: Harcourt, Brace & Co.,
pp. 211, 212, 213.
Brief description of Berryman as an under-
graduate at Columbia, noting his preoccupation with poetry.

<u>1959 A   BOOKS - NONE</u>

<u>1959 B   SHORTER WRITINGS</u>

1   ALVAREZ, A. "Poetry and Poverty," <u>The Observer</u>
[London], (10 May), p. 24.
Review of <u>Homage to Mistress Broadstreet
and Other Poems</u>, and one other volume. Calls
Berryman's verse "intelligent," and notes
that it typically moves "towards some kind of
moral definition." Praises "Homage to Mistress Bradstreet" for its style and subject
matter, and calls it "perhaps the most important poem since 'Four Quartets.'"

2   ARMSTRONG, ROBERT. "Unchartered Territories,"
<u>PoetryR</u>, I (July-September), 175-76.
Brief review of <u>Homage to Mistress Bradstreet and Other Poems</u>.

3   BRACE, KEITH. "Muse Across the Atlantic," Bir-
mingham [England] <u>Post</u> (8 September).
Review of <u>Homage to Mistress Bradstreet
and Other Poems</u>, calling the title poem a

1959

(BRACE, KEITH)
"<u>tour de force</u>" that is almost great, and
noting that "almost anything can be expected
now" of Berryman.

4   CLARKE, AUSTIN. "The Tenth Muse," <u>Irish Times</u>
        (10 October), p. 6.
            Review of <u>Homage to Mistress Bradstreet and
        Other Poems</u>. Describes the title poem and
        calls it a "remarkable experiment."

5   CORKE, HILARY. Review of <u>Homage to Mistress
        Bradstreet and Other Poems</u>, <u>The Listener</u>
        (26 November), 945-46.
            The sensibility revealed in Berryman's
        short poems shows him to be a "good poet,"
        but "Homage to Mistress Bradstreet" is "ro-
        mantic piano concerto stuff."

6   FRASER, G. S. "I, They, We," <u>New Statesman</u>
        (2 May), 614-15.
            Review of <u>Homage to Mistress Bradstreet and
        Other Poems</u> and other volumes. Berryman's
        verse is "studied," his subject the conflict
        between the Puritan tradition and the aes-
        thetic impulse.

7   HOPKINS, KENNETH. "Literary Baggage From All
        Parts," <u>Books and Bookmen</u> (September), 22-23.
            Review of <u>Homage to Mistress Bradstreet and
        Other Poems</u> and eight other books. Berryman's
        verse does not make a significant contribu-
        tion to English poetry.

8   KERMODE, FRANK. "Talent and More," <u>Spectator</u>,
        CCII (1 May), 628.
            Review of <u>Homage to Mistress Bradstreet and
        Other Poems</u> and other books. The title poem
        is a significant work. Although its style

1960

(KERMODE, FRANK)
   appears to be influenced by Hopkins, it prob-
   ably owes more to Edward Taylor and Anne
   Bradstreet.

9   MONTAGUE, JOHN. "American Pegasus," Studies: An
      Irish Quarterly Review, XLVIII (Summer), 183-
      91 [184-85].
         Review of Homage to Mistress Bradstreet and
      Other Poems and other works. Berryman's short
      poems are praiseworthy, and the title poem is
      impressive, although the language succeeds
      only in the childbirth scene.

10   STANFORD, DEREK. "For Other than Poets," Time
      and Tide (29 August), 936-37.
         Review of Homage to Mistress Bradstreet and
      Other Poems and Warren's Promises. Both books
      are strong and original, and meant to be read
      by people "other than poets." The language
      of "Homage to Mistress Bradstreet" is, at its
      best, "taut and rapid."

11   THOMPSON, JOHN. "Poetry Chronicle," Poetry, XCV
      (November), 107-16 [108-10].
         Review of His Thought Made Pockets and the
      Plane Buckt and other books. These poems are
      in the style of Homage to Mistress Bradstreet,
      but are more successful--short poems bear up
      better under the linguistic violence of
      Berryman's style, which projects an "abso-
      lutely authentic" voice.

1960 A   BOOKS

1   BEACH, JOSEPH WARREN. Obsessive Images, edited
      by William Van O'Connor. Minneapolis: Uni-
      versity of Minnesota Press.

1960

(BEACH, JOSEPH WARREN)
Discussion of Berryman's use of some of the "obsessive images" of the poets of the thirties and forties--ceremony, fear, the assassin image, the hero. Berryman's use of them is related to their uses in the work of Yeats and Auden. Discusses only Berryman's early poems--through The Dispossessed. The treatment of Berryman is part of an ongoing critical argument sustained by discussions of the work of a great many poets.

1960 B SHORTER WRITINGS

1 ANON. "Eight in the Arts Cited," New York Times (5 March), p. 17.
    Notice of Berryman's receipt of a $1,500 grant from Brandeis University for poetry.

2 FITZGERALD, ROBERT. "Notes on American Poetry After 1945," The American Review [Bologna], I (Autumn), 127-35 [129-31].
    Through his mastery of language, rhythm and stanza form in Homage to Mistress Bradstreet, Berryman brings the complex emotions of Mistress Bradstreet and the varied "pioneering scene" alive, recovering an American tradition. Berryman "bided his time and made the best poem of his generation."

1961 A BOOKS - NONE

1961 B SHORTER WRITINGS

1 GALLER, DAVID. "Four Poets," SR, LXIX (Winter), 168-74 [172-74].
    Review of His Thought Made Pockets and the Plane Buckt, praising the range of language

1963

(GALLER, DAVID)
and emotions, and noting that Berryman's
personal verse, unlike Lowell's, is written
"from the eye of the storm."

1962 A BOOKS - NONE

1962 B SHORTER WRITINGS

1   FALCK, COLIN. "Dreams and Responsibilities,"
The Review (June-July), 3-18 [9-10].
Review of A. Alvarez, The New Poetry.
Berryman's work is intelligent, but only that.
Other poetic qualities are missing; Berryman's
poems have no "real voice of their own."
(The selection of Berryman's verse in The
New Poetry consists primarily of early poems.)

2   HERZBERG, MAX J. "John Berryman," The Reader's
Encyclopedia of American Literature. New
York: Thomas Y. Crowell, p. 81.
Brief entry, describing Berryman's career.

1963 A BOOKS - NONE

1963 B SHORTER WRITINGS

1   ANON. "Poetry Awards," Ramparts: The National
Catholic Journal, II (May), 4-6 [6].
Brief description of Berryman's dream songs
("there will be seventy-five . . . in the
completed poem") and description of the individual award-winning songs published here.

2   ANON. "News Notes," Poetry, CII (July), 276.
Notice of Berryman's winning $700 first
prize in a poetry competition sponsored by

1963

      (ANON.)
          Ramparts: The National Catholic Journal.
          See also 1963.B1.

3   EVANS, ARTHUR AND CATHERINE EVANS. "Pieter
          Brueghel and John Berryman: Two Winter Land-
          scapes," TSLL, V (Autumn), 310-18.
            Berryman's "Winter Landscape" has the same
          theme as the painting it is based on,
          Brueghel's "Hunters in the Snow": man's iso-
          lation and "his inability to achieve communi-
          ty." The arrangement of stanzas parallels
          the composition of the painting, Berryman's
          diction parallels Brueghel's depiction, and
          the "narrative tempo" of the poem parallels
          the "visual sequence" of the painting.

4   MERAS, PHYLLIS. "John Berryman on Today's Liter-
          ature," Providence Journal (26 May).
            Interview with Berryman in which he notes
          the influence of American poetry abroad, be-
          moans the lack of good literary magazines in
          this country, discusses some current literary
          figures, and briefly describes his dream songs.

5   SPENDER, STEPHEN AND DONALD HALL, EDS. "John
          Berryman," The Concise Encyclopedia of English
          and American Poets. New York: Hawthorne
          Books, 55-56.
            Brief entry, describing Berryman's career,
          noting his style.

1964 A BOOKS - NONE

1964 B SHORTER WRITINGS

1   ANON. Review of 77 Dream Songs, Kirkus Reviews,
          XXXII (15 March), 329.

1964

(ANON.)
> The book is an extraordinary achievement, both "technically and thematically." Its originality and eccentricity will put many readers off, but it is a lasting achievement.

2   ANON. "Twenty Will Get Grants in Arts and Letters," New York Times (5 May), p. 46.
> Notice of Berryman's receipt of the $1,000 Loines Award for poetry from the National Institute for Arts and Letters.

3   ANON. "'U' Prof Honored for Poetry Book by National Institute," Minnesota Daily [University of Minnesota] (7 May), p. 10.
> Announcement of Berryman's receipt of the Loines Award. See also 1964.B2.

4   ANON. Review of 77 Dream Songs, Booklist, LX (15 June), 946–47.
> Brief note, describing the poem.

5   ANON. Review of 77 Dream Songs, Choice, I (July), 176.
> Brief review. The book is difficult, but "wonderful half-nonsense."

6   ALVAREZ, A. "The Joker in the Pack," The Observer [London] (22 November), p. 27.
> Review of 77 Dream Songs. The "joker" is Henry, and most of the jokes are at his expense. This "fragmentary inner biography" is extraordinarily difficult but highly rewarding. The central perception around which Berryman works is "'we are using our skins for wallpaper and we cannot win.'" Reprinted in Beyond All This Fiddle. New York: Random House, 1968, 88–90 (1968.B8).

31

1964

7   BOGAN, LOUISE. "Verse," NY, XL (7 November),
    238-43 [242-43].
        77 Dream Songs reduces language at times to
    a sub-human level. It is "exasperating" in
    its "desperate artificiality."

8   BRINNIN, JOHN MALCOLM. "The Last Minstrel," New
    York Times Book Review (23 August), p. 5.
        Review of 77 Dream Songs. Description of
    the poem, noting that the dream-structure
    makes for some incoherence, but praising the
    technique evidenced in the poem.

9   COTT, JONATHAN. "Theodore Roethke and John Berry-
    man; Two Dream Poets," in On Contemporary
    Literature, edited by Richard Kostelanetz.
    New York: Avon Books, pp. 520-31.
        Although Berryman's unique style is present
    in his earlier works, it is in 77 Dream Songs
    that Berryman finds "the perfect vehicle for
    his style and vision." In that book, exhib-
    iting a profound moral sense, Berryman de-
    scribes the "decline and fall of the con-
    temporary West." Reprinted in Kostelanetz,
    ed. The New American Arts. New York:
    Horizon Press, 1965, pp. 119-28.

10 ELLIOTT, GEORGE P. "Poetry Chronicle," HudR,
    XVII (Autumn), 451-64 [457-58].
        Review of 77 Dream Songs and other books.
    The flamboyant style of the successful songs
    is "exhilarating," but the incoherence and
    obscurity of many is a severe drawback.

11 FULLER, JOHN. "Mr. Berryman Shays His Sing," The
    Guardian (4 December).

12 FURBANK, P. N. "New Poetry," The Listener
(10 December), 949.
Review of 77 Dream Songs and other volumes.
The vitality of the "narcissistic" style is
admirable, and although one can't understand
half the book, the convention of Henry's
"dream-diary" is likeable and the series of
three-stanza songs that constitutes the form
"is a brilliant invention."

13 JOHN, GODFREY. "Old Words Find New Relationships," Christian Science Monitor (30 July),
p. 5.
The style of 77 Dream Songs represents a
"rape of the word" but the poem succeeds in
revealing "'the horror of unlove.'"

14 JOHNSON, CAROL. "John Berryman and Mistress
Bradstreet: A Relation of Reason," Essays
in Criticism, XIV (October), 388-96.
Discussion of Homage to Mistress Bradstreet
concentrating on the effects of the language.
The implication of an archaic speech pattern
is achieved by using a style which gives the
effects of Sprung Rhythm without using the
"technical liberties which it permits." The
poem begins to fail during the unconvincing
central section, in which "symptoms of
hysteria" become more important than the
"crafting of the verse." Reprinted in
Reason's Double Agents. Chapel Hill: University of North Carolina Press, 1966, 105-16.

15 KNOX, SANKA. "Fourteen Join National Arts Institute; Academy Inducts Four," New York Times
(21 May), p. 41.
Notice of Berryman's receipt of the Loines
Award for poetry. See also 1964.B2,B3).

16   LEVENSON, J. C. "Berryman's Dream Songs Combine
        Comic and Terrifying," Minneapolis Tribune
        (7 June), p. 8.
            The comedy in 77 Dream Songs keeps the pain
        from turning into either sentimentality or a
        "merely private nightmare." The poems are
        difficult, but their music, rhyme and above
        all their "moral center" enable the reader to
        get "rational pleasure from these irrational
        songs."

17   LOWELL, ROBERT. "The Poetry of John Berryman,"
        New York Review of Books, II (28 May), 2-3.
            Review of 77 Dream Songs. Description of
        the development of Berryman's style, from
        "The Statue" through 77 Dream Songs. The
        main faults of the Dream Songs are "the threat
        of mannerism" and incoherence, but balancing
        those are Berryman's language and sensibility.
        (In New York Review of Books, II (11 June),
        23, Lowell, in a letter, corrects his descrip-
        tion of Mr. Bones from "one of the characters"
        to Henry.)

18   PRESS, JOHN. "Five Poets," Punch, CCXLVII (30
        December), 1010.
            Review of 77 Dream Songs and other volumes.
        Although there are some successful poems in
        77 Dream Songs, Berryman's stylistic "tricks"
        are "maddening and unsatisfying."

19   RICH, ADRIENNE. "Mr. Bones, He Lives," Nation,
        CXCVIII (25 May), 538, 40.
            Review of 77 Dream Songs. Berryman, through
        his use of personae in this original and
        beautiful book, manages to move toward the
        dramatic without losing the lyric voice. The
        book is unified by the character of Henry,

(RICH, ADRIENNE)
who is "bruised, raging and fiendishly intelligent" at the same time.

20   SLAVITT, DAVID. "Deep Soundings and Surface
Noises," Book Week [New York Herald Tribune]
(10 May), p. 14.
Review of 77 Dream Songs and other books.
Both in theory and in practice, the notion of
Henry, the use of the minstrel show and the
dialect are "absurd." Berryman is "simply
slumming."

21   SMITH, RAY. Review of 77 Dream Songs, LJ, LXXXIX
(15 June), 2622.
In a style reminiscent of Homage to Mistress
Bradstreet, the volume "recreates poetry,"
allowing it to enter into "contemporary dis-
course."

22   SMITH, WILLIAM JAY. "Pockets of Thought,"
Harpers, CCXXIX (August), 100-02.
77 Dream Songs may have been influenced by
Lowell's Life Studies in the same way that
Homage to Mistress Bradstreet was influenced
by Lowell's earlier work. The title is
ironic: there are more nightmares here than
dreams, and the three-stanza sections don't
resemble songs. Berryman's literary ancestor
is Poe--his subject is the "nightmare of
existence."

23   STITT, PETER A. "John, Henry, and Mr. Bones,"
Ivory Tower [University of Minnesota] (1 June),
36-37.
The poem is influenced, but certainly not
derivative; although it is personal, it is
more than autobiographical. The mixture of
so many kinds of language in the poem is a

1964

(STITT, PETER A.)
great accomplishment, and although the syntax
is often difficult, it is logical, and "a
little care" in reading will clear up the
problems.

1965 A BOOKS - NONE

1965 B SHORTER WRITINGS

1   ANON. "American Poetry's Casual Look," London
        Times (7 January), p. 13.
        77 Dream Songs is not an easy book, but it
        does "evoke an extraordinary range of feelings"
        and shows Berryman to be a gifted poet.

2   ANON. "Arts Institute Names Thirteen for Note-
        worthy Creative Work," New York Times (9
        February), p. 34.
        Notice of Berryman's election to the
        National Institute of Arts and Letters.

3   ANON. "Zoo-Maze: The World in Vaudeville," TLS,
        LXIV (15 April), 292.
        Review of 77 Dream Songs. Notes that the
        poem is suffused with a "nostalgia for an
        ordered but not inhuman stability." Much of
        the review is taken up by a convincing and
        coherent summary of the "plot" of the poem,
        describing Henry's movement from "heartbreak
        and a sense of sterility" to a sober, "nega-
        tive courage."

4   ANON. "John Berryman," New York Times (4 May),
        p. 39.
        Brief description of Berryman's career,
        occasioned by his winning the Pulitzer Prize.

1965

5   ANON. "The Pulitzer Prize," <u>New York Times</u>
        (4 May), p. 42.
          Editorial on the Pulitzer Prizes, noting
        that the only sign of interest by the Pulitzer
        committee in "more experimental writing" is
        the "well-merited" award to Berryman.

6   ANON. "Pulitzer Prize Once a 'Nothing' to Him;
        Now Berryman's Happy to Accept," Minneapolis
        <u>Star</u> (4 May), p. 18D.
          Description of the Berryman household on
        the occasion of Berryman's winning the
        Pulitzer Prize for <u>77 Dream Songs</u>. Quotes
        Berryman as saying that "he expects to finish
        the rest of the poem within a year."

7   ANON. "<u>77 Dream Songs</u> Wins Pulitzer Prize,"
        <u>Minnesota Daily</u> [University of Minnesota]
        (4 May), p. 1.
          Notes receipt of the prize, quotes the re-
        sponses of Ralph Ross and Allen Tate.

8   ANON. "'U' Professor Awarded Pulitzer Poetry
        Prize," Minneapolis <u>Tribune</u> (4 May), pp. 1, 6.
          Brief description of Berryman's career.
        Quotes Berryman as saying that the complete
        <u>Dream Songs</u> will contain 161 songs and will
        be finished within a year.

9   ARMS, GEORGE. "American Poetry," in <u>Encyclopedia</u>
        <u>of Poetry and Poetics</u>, edited by Alex Premin-
        ger. Princeton: Princeton University Press,
        pp. 23-31 [31].
          Very brief discussion of <u>Homage to Mistress</u>
        <u>Bradstreet</u>.

1965

10 BENET, WILLIAM R. "John Berryman," Reader's
        Encyclopedia. Vol. 2. 2nd ed. New York:
        Thomas Y. Crowell, p. 101.
            Very brief entry, describing Berryman's
        career.

11 BENJAMIN, PHILIP. "'Subject Was Roses' Wins
        Pulitzer Prize for Drama," New York Times
        (4 May), pp. 1, 39 [39].
            Notice of Berryman's winning the Pulitzer
        Prize for 77 Dream Songs.

12 BERRYMAN, JOHN. "One Answer to a Question,"
        Shenandoah, XVII (Autumn), 67–76.
            Berryman describes the changes in his work
        from his early years to the present, dis-
        cussing the early influences of Yeats and
        Auden, the strategy of leaving things out of
        a poem in "Winter Landscape," the beginning of
        the use of the "ambiguous pronoun" in "The
        Ball Poem," and the subjects, forms and
        styles of Homage to Mistress Bradstreet and
        the dream songs. Reprinted as "Changes" in
        Poets on Poetry, edited by Howard Nemerov.
        New York: Basic Books, 1966, pp. 94–103.

13 BORNHAUSER, FRED. "Poetry by the Poem," VQR, XLI
        (Winter), 146–52 [148–49].
            Review of 77 Dream Songs and other volumes.
        Brief description of Berryman's "spontaneous
        and staggering verses."

14 _____. "77 Dream Songs," in Masterplots Annual,
        1965, edited by Frank Magill. New York:
        Salem Press, pp. 275–77.
            Brief description of the difficulties and
        the rewards to be found in the volume, which
        "titillates . . . teases . . . and glorifies."

15   COTT, JONATHAN. "The New Poetry," in <u>The New</u>
<u>American Arts</u>, edited by Richard Kostelanetz.
New York: Horizon Press, pp. 119-28.
    Discussion of Berryman is a reprint of
"Theodore Roethke and John Berryman: Two
Dream Poets," in <u>On Contemporary Literature</u>,
edited by Richard Kostelanetz (1964.B9), q. v.

16   CURRAN, MARY DOYLE. "Poems Public and Private,"
<u>MR</u>, VI (Winter-Spring), 411-15 [414-15].
    The style of <u>77 Dream Songs</u> is mere manner-
ism. The blackface dialect is "in bad taste,"
and the poems are without feeling. After
figuring out the literary puzzles in the
poems, one is simply left with a "feeling
of dissipation and boredom."

17   DAVISON, PETER. "Madness in the New Poetry,"
<u>Atlantic</u>, CCXV (January), 90-93 [91].
    Review of <u>77 Dream Songs</u> and other volumes.
The handling of the stanzas and the use of
language are admirable; the disorderliness,
"the perversity, the self-pity" are not.

18   DICKEY, JAMES. "Orientations," <u>ASch</u>, XXXIV
(Autumn), 646-58 [646-48].
    Review of <u>77 Dream Songs</u> and other works.
Berryman, who is "very nearly a great poet,"
creates a "magnificently unnatural style" and
provides an exhilarating experience for the
reader through his language. Reprinted in
<u>Babel to Byzantium</u>. New York: Farrar,
Straus and Giroux, 1968, pp. 198-99 (1968.B16).

19   GARRIGUE, JEAN. "Language Noble, Witty and Wild,"
<u>New Leader</u>, XLVIII (15 February), 23-24.
    Review of <u>77 Dream Songs</u> and other volumes.
The style of the book is especially praise-
worthy; the songs "skin language to the bone"
to describe Henry's condition.

1965

20   GHOSE, ZULFIKAR. Review of 77 Dream Songs, Ambit,
         XXIII (1965), 45–46.
             Berryman's curiously distorted language is
         the source of his originality, and it calls
         forth an extraordinary range of emotions. If
         read just a few at a time, the songs seem
         obscure; they should be read as a whole, in a
         single sitting.

21   GLAUBER, ROBERT H. "The Poet's Intention," PrS,
         XXXIX (Fall), 276–80 [279–80].
             Review of 77 Dream Songs and other volumes.
         Praises the language of the volume, noting
         the mixture of comedy and tragedy in it as
         well as its "universality."

22   HAMILTON, IAN. "John Berryman," London Magazine,
         IV ns (February), 93–100.
             Discussion of the development of Berryman's
         poetry from his early poems to 77 Dream Songs.
         Analyzes "The Disciple," "The Statue," and
         "The Traveler," noting the somewhat disturbing
         conflict between the style and the "rather
         trite solemnities" of statement in the poems.
         Describes the influence of Edward Taylor's
         style in Homage to Mistress Bradstreet, and
         the "silly relish" Berryman takes in syntactic
         inversions in 77 Dream Songs. Describes
         Henry as less a character than a collection
         of gestures, and notes that one must rifle
         the book for "flashes" of memorable writing.
         Reprinted in A Poetry Chronicle. New York:
         Harper & Row, 1973, pp. 111–21 (1973.B30).

23   HART, JAMES D. "John Berryman," in The Oxford
         Companion to American Literature. New York:
         Oxford University Press, p. 75.
             Brief description of Berryman's career.

24   JACKSON, BRUCE. "Berryman's Chaplinesque," MinnR,
         V (January-April), 90-94.
              In autobiographical writing, such as 77
         Dream Songs, one must make one's self inter-
         esting enough to be worth the reading, and
         Berryman certainly does that. Berryman's
         idea of using a "shlemeil" as a protagonist
         is new in American poetry, and very effective:
         Henry serves as a "refractor" of a mad world.

25   LUNDEGAARD, BOB. "Song of a Poet: John Berryman,"
         Minneapolis Tribune (27 June), pp. 1E-2E.
              Interview with Berryman, in which he dis-
         cusses his methods of composition, his career,
         and the dream songs.

26   MARTZ, LOUIS. "Recent Poetry: The Elegiac Mode,"
         YR, LIV (Winter), 285-98 [285-86].
              Review of 77 Dream Songs and other volumes,
         noting the elegiac tone of Berryman's volume,
         and "the cleverly dislocated language" of the
         poem.

27   MEREDITH, WILLIAM. "Henry Tasting All the Secret
         Bits of Life: Berryman's Dream Songs," WSCL,
         VI (Winter-Spring), 27-33.
              Early and important essay on 77 Dream Songs,
         concentrating on the character of Henry.
         Henry is a man of many selves, a self-con-
         scious imaginary Negro and imaginary madman.
         The discovery of his identity, "by him and by
         us, comprises the plot of the poem."

28   MORSE, SAMUEL FRENCH. "Poetry, 1964," WSCL, VI
         (Autumn), 354-67 [360].
              Brief review of 77 Dream Songs, describing
         the poem as "an achievement," albeit "a
         baffling one."

John Berryman: A Reference Guide

29 PEARSON, GABRIEL. "John Berryman—Poet as
    Medium," The Review, XV (April), 3-17.
    Berryman's poetry is a mediumistic attempt
    to take on a multiplicity of voices, and by
    so doing, create a self. Reprinted in The
    Modern Poet, edited by Ian Hamilton. New
    York: Horizon Press, 1969, 111-24 (1969.B45).

30 RICKS, CHRISTOPHER. "Desperate Hours," New States-
    man, LXIX (15 January), 79-80.
    Review of 77 Dream Songs and other volumes.
    The volume contains some excellent individual
    songs, but many unsuccessful ones as well,
    especially the satirical and religious songs.

31 ROSENTHAL, M. L. "The Couch and Poetic Insight,"
    Reporter, XXXII (25 March), 52-54.
    With 77 Dream Songs, Berryman joins the
    confessional movement, although he is not a
    good enough poet to be considered the equal
    of Lowell. About twenty of the 77 songs
    stand out, largely because of the successful
    style, but the volume points up the dangers
    that future poets may succumb to, if they
    assume that "every nuance of suffering" is a
    new poetic insight. Reprinted as a part of
    "Other Confessional Poets," in The New Poets.
    New York: Oxford University Press, 1967,
    pp. 118-30 (1967.B25), q.v.

32 S., D. H. Review of 77 Dream Songs, Dublin Maga-
    zine, IV (Spring), 84-86.
    There are bits of good poetry here, but they
    don't add up to anything significant. Berry-
    man is much too "self-indulgent," "at the
    expense of the reader," and as a result, 77
    Dream Songs is not nearly as interesting or
    as good a poem as Homage to Mistress Brad-
    street.

33   SEIDEL, FREDERICK. "Berryman's Dream Songs,"
        Poetry, CV (January), 257-59.
           Review of _77 Dream Songs_. Read as a whole,
        the songs make more sense than when read in-
        dividually--they gloss one another. Berry-
        man's rhythm is admirable, as is the humor
        of these songs and their language. The chief
        fault is that some lines don't work, and
        simply seem irrelevant.

34   SERGEANT, HOWARD. "Poetry Review," _English_, XV
        (Spring), 154-57 [154].
           Brief review of _77 Dream Songs_ and many
        other books. Praises the originality of the
        language.

35   STEVENS, E. Review of _77 Dream Songs_, _Books and
        Bookmen_, X (January), 27.
           Brief note, describing the favorable criti-
        cal reception the book has had.

36   STRICKHAUSEN, HARRY. "Ancient Signs, Infamous
        Characters, New Rhythms," _North American Re-
        view_, CCL (Spring), 59-60.
           Review of _77 Dream Songs_, noting the juxta-
        positions of serious and comic matter, Henry's
        friend, and the mad world that Berryman de-
        scribes. The volume as a whole, however, is
        "too dense, too allusive" to be completely
        successful.

37   TOYNBEE, PHILLIP. "Berryman's Songs," _Encounter_,
        XXIV (March), 76-78.
           Review of _77 Dream Songs_. Berryman is "an
        immediately appetizing poet," but closer
        examination shows that there is less in his
        work than there appears to be. His humor is
        puerile, his sentiments trite. His poetry
        can be readily imitated. His chief

1965

(TOYNBEE, PHILLIP)
accomplishment, like Pound's, may lie in his
having opened up stylistic realms that later,
better poets might explore.

38   WIGGIN, MAURICE. "Boredom Becomes Exhilaration,"
Sunday Times [London] (3 January), p. 33.
Adjective-filled review of 77 Dream Songs
and other volumes. The "enormous vim and
zest" of Berryman's style is exhilarating and
addictive. Berryman is "a boredom-banishing
magician."

39   WILSON, EDMUND. The Bit Between My Teeth. New
York: Farrar, Straus and Giroux, 548n-549n.
Note that includes Berryman among the
writers Wilson admires, because of the im-
posing "poetic personality" presented in 77
Dream Songs.

40   WOODS, JOHN. "Five Poets," Shenandoah, XVI
(Spring), 85-91 [87-89].
77 Dream Songs is "one of the most important
books of the year;" the technique that Berryman has found is so liberating, however, that
it creates a danger--the poem could go on for-
ever. Berryman must find the discipline necessary to bring order to such an open form.

1966 A BOOKS - NONE

1966 B SHORTER WRITINGS

1   ANON. "'U' Poet Wins Guggenheim Fellowship,"
Minneapolis Tribune (4 April), p. 47.
Notice of Berryman's receipt of the Guggen-
heim for creative writing in poetry, which
Berryman said he would spend in Ireland.

2   BERRYMAN, JOHN. "Changes," in <u>Poets on Poetry</u>,
     edited by Howard Nemerov. New York: Basic
     Books, pp. 94-103.
          Reprint of "One Answer to a Question,"
     <u>Shenandoah</u>, XVII (Autumn), 67-76 (1965.B12),
     q.v.

3   DONADIO, STEPHEN. "Some Younger Poets in America,"
     in <u>Modern Occasions</u>, edited by Philip Rahv.
     New York: Farrar, Straus and Giroux.
          Notes that <u>77 Dream Songs</u> resembles Beat
     poetry more closely than it resembles Academic
     poetry.

4   ETHERIDGE, JAMES M. AND BARBARA KAPOLA. "John
     Berryman," <u>Contemporary Authors, XV-XVI</u>.
     Detroit: Gale Research Co., pp. 43-44.
          Brief description of Berryman's career and
     critical responses to Berryman's major works.

5   GILBERT, ISABELLE S. Review of <u>77 Dream Songs</u>,
     <u>Chicago Jewish Forum</u>, XXIV (Summer), 325-26.
          <u>77 Dream Songs</u> is too avant-garde: the
     linguistic experiments hamper communication.
     As an experimentalist, Berryman is subtle and
     inventive, "but it doesn't seem necessary to
     belabor the poetry reader with obscurities."

6   GIRRI, ALBERTO. "John Berryman," <u>Quince Poetas
     Norteamericanos</u>. Buenos Aires: Bibliografica
     Omeba, pp. 101-19.
          Describes Berryman's career, noting that
     although Berryman's concern with the technical
     aspects of verse enabled him to write some
     excellent poems early in his career, it was
     not until <u>Homage to Mistress Bradstreet</u> and
     <u>77 Dream Songs</u>, in which Berryman formed a
     language equal to his sensibility, that he
     was able to reach a high level of achievement.

1966

7   GULLANS, CHARLES. "Edgar Bowers' The Astronomers
        and Other New Verse," SoR, II (Winter), 189–
        209 [196–97].
          77 Dream Songs is a trivial book, not a
        volume of poetry at all, but a collection of
        "notes for short stories."

8   HUGHES, DANIEL. "The Dream Songs: Spells for
        Survival," SoRA, II (1966), 5–17.
          77 Dream Songs represents the same kind of
        breakthrough for Berryman that Life Studies
        represented for Lowell. The germ of the
        Dream Songs can be found in Berryman's com-
        ments on Crane's poetry: "they are like
        things just seen and said, said for use."
        Henry is not simply a mask for Berryman, but
        a vehicle who can take on whatever identities
        the poem requires, and thus becomes Everyman.

9   JOHNSON, CAROL. "John Berryman and Mistress Brad-
        street: A Relation of Reason," Reason's
        Double Agents. Chapel Hill: University of
        North Carolina Press, pp. 105–16.
          Reprinted from Essays in Criticism, XIV
        (October, 1964), 388–96 (1964.B14), q.v.

10   RAMSEY, PAUL. "In Exasperation and Gratitude,"
        SR, LXXIV (Autumn), 930–45 [936–38].
          Review of 77 Dream Songs and other books.
        Notes that there are few completely success-
        ful songs, but that nevertheless, largely be-
        cause of "the Henry idiom," it is "exciting
        poetry."

11   SHEPARD, RICHARD F. "Berryman Named for Poetry
        Prize," New York Times (29 October), p. 29.
          Brief description of Berryman's career, and
        notice of his winning the $5,000 Academy of
        American Poets Fellowship.

12 SISSON, JONATHAN. "My Whiskers Fly: An Interview
With John Berryman," Ivory Tower [University
of Minnesota] (3 October), 14-18, 34-35.
Most of the interview is concerned with the
Dream Songs, then still planned to number 161
(although at the time of the interview 181
had been written and preserved). The relationship between Henry and Berryman is discussed,
especially in relation to the last song, and
Berryman talks about the "secretiveness" of
the Dream Songs, along with many other topics.

1967 A BOOKS - NONE

1967 B SHORTER WRITINGS

1 ANON. "Poet at 'U' Wins $5,000 Award," Minneapo-
lis Tribune (1 January), p. 9.
Notice of Berryman's receipt of the 1966
Fellowship of the Academy of American Poets.

2 ANON. Review of Berryman's Sonnets, Kirkus Reviews, XXXV (1 March), 306.
The book is interesting because of the insights it provides into the development of
Berryman's style. It is occasionally "charming," but not "memorable Berryman."

3 ANON. Review of Berryman's Sonnets, Booklist,
LXIII (1 June), 1027.
Brief review, noting that many of the Sonnets are awkward, but that the volume will be
of interest as a contrast to Berryman's later,
better work.

4 ANON. Review of Berryman's Sonnets, Beloit Poetry
Journal, XVII (Summer), 34.
Brief note describing the Sonnets.

1967

5   ANON. Review of <u>Berryman's Sonnets</u>, <u>VQR</u>, XLIII
       (Autumn), clxix.
          The <u>Sonnets</u> are a difficult "game," and a
       "grand parody of traditional form."

6   ANON. Review of <u>Short Poems</u>, <u>Publisher's Weekly</u>,
       CXCII (2 October), 52.
          Brief review, noting that Berryman is
       "never obscure" and that he finds "signifi-
       cance in the commonplace."

7   ANON. Review of <u>Short Poems</u>, <u>Kirkus Reviews</u>,
       XXXV (15 October), 1301.
          While there are some fine poems here, most
       of Berryman's early work is as "tiresome as
       yesterday's headlines." He will be remem-
       bered for his later work, not for these poems.

8   ANON. "Berryman Gets $10,000 Award," Minneapolis
       <u>Tribune</u> (17 November), p. 1.
          Notice of Berryman's winning an award for
       "distinguished service to American letters"
       from the National Endowment for the Humani-
       ties. Berryman's response briefly recorded.

9   ANON. "News Notes," <u>Poetry</u>, CXI (December),
       206–07.
          Notes that Berryman was poet-in-residence
       at Trinity College (Rhode Island) during the
       week of October 9. <u>See also</u> 1967.B10.

10   BERKMAN, FLORENCE. "Pulitzer Poet Visiting at
       Trinity This Week," Hartford [Conn.] <u>Times</u>
       (11 October), p. 14G.
          Interview occasioned by Berryman's visit
       to Trinity College as poet-in-residence for
       a week. Berryman discusses the difficulty

(BERKMAN, FLORENCE)
> of his poetry, the difficulties of life in
> the modern world.

11   BEWLEY, MARIUS. "Poetry Chronicle," HudR, XX
>   (August), 500-04.
>   Close examination of the failings of Berry-
> man's Sonnets: the lack of development of
> Lise as a character, the self-conscious 'lit-
> erary' quality of the poem, the ineffective
> inversions of the style. Notes that the prob-
> able source of Sonnet 44 is Donne's "The Can-
> onization," and the probable source of Sonnet
> 28 is Stefan Zweig's biography of Balzac.

12   CUSHMAN, JEROME. Review of Short Poems, LJ, LX
>   (15 November), 4162.
>   Brief review, noting some of the themes of
> Berryman's early work, for example his concern
> with the pain of love, and his interest in
> portraying inner turmoil.

13   DONALDSON, SCOTT. "Berryman's Poems Span 40
>   Years," Minneapolis Tribune (24 December),
>   p. 4.
>   Review of Short Poems. Notes that Berry-
> man's style has changed during the course of
> his career, but his themes, especially "his
> sensitivity to the wounds of life," have not.

14   FELDMAN, BURTON. "John Berryman: Berryman's
>   Sonnets," Denver Quarterly, II (Spring),
>   168-69.
>   Berryman's Sonnets, like his other work,
> raise the question of how much his reputation
> is based on actual achievement and how much
> is based on "his experimental drive." Berry-
> man's language might open up new directions

1967

(FELDMAN, BURTON)
for other poets, but he "can't quite seem to
make poems" out of it.

15   FULLER, EDMUND. "The Bookshelf: Poets of Affir-
mation," Wall Street Journal (24 May), p. 16.
Brief description of Berryman's Sonnets,
noting that Lise, unlike Shakespeare's her-
oine, is "a bright lady."

16   _____. "The Bookshelf: Quartet of Masters Tops
Big Poetry Crop," Wall Street Journal
(27 December), p. 8.
Brief review of Short Poems, describing the
volume.

17   GELPI, ALBERT. "Early Poems by Berryman," Christian Science Monitor (20 July), p. 5.
Although Berryman's Sonnets are unsuccess-
ful as a sequence--the emotions are "too raw"
and the language "too restless"--they contain
some fine individual lyrics and illustrate
the fact that Berryman was looking for a sustained form early in his career.

18   HOWARD, JANE. "Whiskey and Ink, Whiskey and Ink,"
Life, LXIII (21 July), 67-76.
Notice that, in the words of a colleague
quoted in the article, Berryman "has arrived."
Brief description of Berryman's life and work.
Interview includes Berryman's comments on the
importance of marriage and children, fear and
survival, Francis Chichester, and other topics.
Pictures of Berryman in Irish pubs.

19   JACOBSEN, JOSEPHINE. "Two New Volumes of Poetry,"
Baltimore Evening Sun (8 June), p. 20A.
Review of Berryman's Sonnets and one other
volume. Despite Berryman's talent, evidenced

(JACOBSEN, JOSEPHINE)
by his more recent verse, the Sonnets are "a
dreary and prolonged mistake," too long and
full of flat language.

20 MAZZOCCO, ROBERT. "Harlequin in Hell," New York
Review of Books (29 June), 12-16.
Essay-review of Berryman's Sonnets, which
discusses Homage to Mistress Bradstreet and
77 Dream Songs as well. Berryman is not a
profound poet; "his strengths are in small
moments." But he is a poet whose personality
speaks to our condition. The Sonnets are "a
stumbling breakthrough" to the achievement of
his later poems.

21 MEREDITH, WILLIAM. "Love's Progress," New York
Times Book Review (7 May), p. 8.
Review of Berryman's Sonnets. Description
of the poem, briefly noting the resemblances
to Petrarch's and Shakespeare's sequences and
stating that the technique of the Dream Songs
is evidenced in these early poems.

22 MURRAY, MICHELE. "Music to Dance to, Words to
Ponder," National Catholic Reporter (23 August), 9.
Berryman's Sonnets are difficult and complex because the emotions they are dealing
with are difficult and complex. The language
of the poems is especially praiseworthy--
Berryman pushes "syntax beyond its accepted
borders."

23 NUSSBAUM, ELIZABETH. "Berryman and Tate: Poets
Extraordinaire," Minnesota Daily [University
of Minnesota] (9 November), pp. 7-10.
Interview, concentrating on Berryman's so-
journ in Ireland and memories of the more

1967

(NUSSBAUM, ELIZABETH)
distant past, such as his friendship with
Dylan Thomas.

24   PRYCE-JONES, ALAN. "An Exception to the Rule on
Poets," New York World Journal Tribune (27
April), p. 29.
Brief review of Berryman's Sonnets, de-
scribing the poem.

25   ROSENTHAL, M. L. "Other Confessional Poets," The
New Poets: American and British Poetry Since
World War II. New York: Oxford University
Press, pp. 118-30.
Reprints and expands "The Couch and Poetic
Insight," Reporter, XXXII (25 March, 1965),
52-54 (1965.B31), q.v. Despite the felici-
ties of language in 77 Dream Songs and Berryman's "admirable range and flexibility,"
there is too much chaff in the book for it to
be considered a major work. Homage to Mistress Bradstreet, despite some affectations
in style and the sentimentality of the narrative, is more successful--Berryman is better
able to "objectify his feelings" in that poem.

26   SHAPIRO, KARL. "Showdown at City of Poetry,"
Chicago Sun-Times Book Week (3 December).
Review of Short Poems and other books.
Very brief description of the book, noting
that it traces Berryman's development.

27   SHEPARD, RICHARD F. "Fledgling Poets Get Federal
Help," New York Times (12 December), p. 43.
Notice of Berryman's winning a $10,000
award from the National Council on the Arts
"for his contribution to American Letters."
See also 1967.B8.

28   SHERMAN, JOHN K. "Poet Creates Own Language,"
         Minneapolis Star (5 December), p. 8B.
           Review of Short Poems, concentrating on the
         difficulties and pleasures of Berryman's
         language, which, like paint in an abstract
         painting, is "flung, not written."

29   STAFFORD, W. "Supporting a Reputation," Chicago
         Tribune Books Today (14 May), p. 9.
           Review of Berryman's Sonnets and one other
         book. Even in such a formal setting as a
         sonnet sequence, Berryman is able to provide
         surprise.

30   STEPANCHEV, STEPHEN. "For an Excellent Lady,"
         New Leader, L (22 May), 26-28.
           Berryman's Sonnets are "fascinating and
         disturbing" as a chronicle of overwhelming
         passion. Berryman's stylistic idiosyncracies
         mar the poems, but the sequence contains some
         admirable poetry nonetheless.

31   STITT, PETER A. "Berryman's Vein Profound,"
         MinnR, VII (no. 4), 356-59.
           Review of Berryman's Sonnets, noting that
         the real subject of the poem is the tension
         between Berryman's love for his mistress and
         the moral laws forbidding adulterous love.
         "The theme of evil" unifies the book.

32   TURCO, LEWIS. "Of Laureates and Lovers," SatR,
         L (14 October), 31-33 [31].
           Briefly notes the youthful passion of
         Berryman's Sonnets, and laments the loss of
         that passion in his more recent work.

33   WALSH, CHAD. "A Garland of Poets: Torrid, Ele-
         gant, Ascetic," Chicago Tribune Book World
         (10 September), p. 18.

1967

(WALSH, CHAD)
Describes Berryman's Sonnets as an "uneven"
sequence, the major faults being that Berryman is too heavily influenced and that Lise
is not a fully realized character.

34 WARING, WALTER. Review of Berryman's Sonnets,
LJ, LX (1 April), 1496.
The volume is successful in both its style
and its use of the sonnet sequence form.

1968 A BOOKS

1 CLARK, VIRGINIA PRESCOTT. "The Syntax of John
Berryman's Homage to Mistress Bradstreet."
Ph.D. dissertation, University of Connecticut.
Two analytical methods are applied to the
syntax--analysis of sentence components and a
transformational-generative analysis. Although critics have noted the many syntactic
oddities in the poem, analysis shows that
most occur "within the framework of the normal
English sentence pattern." Indeed, an analysis of the surface structure through a chart
of word order indicates that the poem is a
great deal simpler syntactically than has been
supposed. Syntactic variations lead the reader to an expectation of difficulties and the
feeling that they are more prevalent than
they actually are. What critics have not
noted is the "extensive amount of simplicity
in the poem," which provides the background
that makes the deviations more noticeable.
What deviations there are, serve thematic
functions: as the characters in the poem are
alienated, so too is their language, and since
the poem is concerned with rebellion, it is
appropriate that the language should be re-
bellious.

1968 B   SHORTER WRITINGS

1   ANON. "Tortured Tryst," <u>TLS</u>, LXVII (4 July),
         699.
             Review of Berryman's <u>Sonnets</u>. Brief com-
         parison of the <u>Sonnets</u> and Meredith's <u>Modern
         Love</u>, noting that Berryman's language goes
         far beyond Meredith's innovations. The prob-
         lem with the <u>Sonnets</u> is that the marvelous
         language is used in the service of trivial
         material—Berryman does not succeed in gen-
         eralizing his subject. Reprinted in <u>TLS:
         Essays and Reviews From the Times Literary
         Supplement</u>, 1968. London: Oxford University
         Press, 1969, pp. 103-04.

2   ANON. "Professor Wins Poetry Prize," Minneapolis
         <u>Star</u> (11 July), p. 5B.
             Notice of Berryman's winning the Emily
         Clark Balch Prize of $500 from the Virginia
         Quarterly Review for "Eleven Dream Songs."

3   ANON. Review of <u>His Toy, His Dream, His Rest</u>,
         <u>Publisher's Weekly</u>, CXCIV (9 September), 57.
             Brief note, describing Berryman's work as
         "difficult but authentic."

4   ANON. Review of <u>His Toy, His Dream, His Rest</u>,
         <u>Kirkus Reviews</u>, XXXVI (15 September), 1077-
         78.
             The dream songs are astonishing experiments
         with language, but can only be said to be
         partially successful, for there is no "exhil-
         arating cohesion" to them.

5   ANON. "John Berryman, 'U' Poet, Honored," Min-
         neapolis <u>Star</u> (11 November), p. 10A.
             Notice of Berryman's receiving the $500
         McKnight Prize in literature for <u>Berryman's
         Sonnets</u>.

6   ANON. "Ten of Particular Significance and Excel-
        lence in 1968," New York Times Book Review
        (1 December), p. 1.
           Brief description of His Toy, His Dream,
        His Rest as one of the 'ten best', noting its
        achievement as "nakedly personal" poetry.

7   ALVAREZ, A. "Bottom Drawer," The Observer [Lon-
        don] (5 May), p. 26.
           Review of Berryman's Sonnets, noting that
        in these poems Berryman "served his appren-
        ticeship" in his mature style. Although in
        many ways the poems are dated as a "forties
        performance," at the same time there are
        notes of "authentic Berryman" twenty years
        ahead of its time.

8   _____. "John Berryman," Beyond All This Fiddle.
        New York: Random House, pp. 88-90.
           Reprints "The Joker in the Pack," The
        Observer (22 November, 1964), p. 27 (1964.B6),
        q. v.

9   BERG, MARTIN. "New Berryman Book Continues Dream
        Songs," Minnesota Daily [University of Min-
        nesota] (5 December), pp. 21, 24.
           Berryman's second volume of dream songs is
        even better than the first: it is less
        obscure and there is a more clearly distin-
        guishable continuity between individual songs.

10   BLAND, PETER. "Poetry," London Magazine, VIII ns
        (August), 97-99 [98-99].
           Review of Berryman's Sonnets and one other
        volume. Brief description of the sequence,
        noting the technical successes of Berryman's
        verse.

11   BOGAN, LOUISE. "Verse," NY, XLIV (30 March),
         133-38 [137].
             Brief note describing Short Poems and
         Berryman's Sonnets.

12   BURNS, GERALD. "U. S. Poetry 1967--The Books That
         Matter," SWR, LIII (Winter), 101-06 [104].
             Review of Short Poems and other volumes.
         Brief note, describing the book as "a delight."

13   CARRUTH, HAYDEN. "Declining Occasions," Poetry,
         CXII (May), 119-21.
             Review of Berryman's Sonnets. The roots of
         the style of the dream songs are to be found
         in these sonnets which, perhaps because they
         deal with a real and urgent situation, seem
         to speak with more "artistic urgency" than
         the later poems do.

14   COURTNEY, WINIFRED F., ED. "Berryman, John," The
         Reader's Advisor: A Guide to the Best in
         Literature. New York: R. R. Bowker, pp.
         227-28.
             Brief biography of Berryman and quotations
         from selected criticism.

15   CUSHMAN, JEROME. Review of His Toy, His Dream,
         His Rest, LJ, LXI (15 October), 3791.
             Brief review emphasizing the religious
         element in the dream songs.

16   DICKEY, JAMES. "John Berryman," Babel to Byzan-
         tium. New York: Farrar, Straus and Giroux,
         198-99.
             Reprints "Orientations," ASch, XXXIV
         (Autumn, 1965), pp. 646-58 [646-48]
         (1965.B18), q. v.

1968

17   DODSWORTH, MARTIN. "Agonistes," The Listener
      (9 May), 612.
          Berryman's Sonnets are "more personal" and
      "more accessible" than his other work, and
      assure his place as one of "the major poets
      of our time." The apparently effortless
      language play in the sequence gives the read-
      er a sense of a man obsessed by both love and
      language.

18   FAUCHEREAU, SERGE. "De Lowell à Wilbur par Berry-
      man," Lecture de la Poésie Américaine. Paris:
      Les Editions de Minuit, pp. 149-74.
          General discussion of Berryman's work, from
      the beginning to 77 Dream Songs. Berryman's
      Sonnets mark a transition for Berryman from
      the varying themes and forms of the poems of
      The Dispossessed to a single form and a single
      theme forming a narrative. In 77 Dream Songs,
      Berryman seems to have found his form--by
      adopting the mask of Henry, he can move beyond
      his personal life to consider a vast range of
      material. The problem with the form, how-
      ever, is that there doesn't seem to be any
      reason for the poem to end. Like Merrill
      Moore writing sonnets, Berryman may spend the
      rest of his life writing dream songs.

19   FRASER, G. S. "A Pride of Poets," PR, XXXV (Sum-
      mer), 467-74.
          Review of Short Poems and other volumes.
      Berryman's earlier work, unlike his more
      recent poems, is heavily influenced, and does
      not utilize the "casual strengths of American
      spoken speech."

20   GARRIGUE, JEAN. "Rapidly Shifting States of
      Mind," New Leader, LI (2 December), 13-14.

1968

(GARRIGUE, JEAN)
   Review of His Toy, His Dream, His Rest,
   praising the style and the "authority" of the
   songs, finding the "thematic parenthesis"
   which holds the songs together to be Henry's
   concern with loss and death.

21   GILMAN, MILTON.   "Berryman and the Sonnets,"
        Chelsea, XXII/XXIII (June), 158-69.
        The central concern of Berryman's Sonnets
   is the speaker's "increasingly complex psycho-
   logical state," as the narrative takes the
   reader from Berryman's early involvement with
   his mistress to his final separation from her.
   The early poems are literary and "artificial,"
   the later ones direct and colloquial, re-
   flecting Berryman's movement from "idealiza-
   tion to realization of his subject."

22   GRANT, DAMIAN.   "Centre Court," The Tablet,
        CCXXII (6 July), 673-74.
        Review of Berryman's Sonnets and other books.
   In Grant's tennis tournament metaphor, American
   poets frequently play on "the centre court of
   English poetry;" Berryman is seeded number one.

23   HOWES, VICTOR.   "More Dream Songs," Christian
        Science Monitor (5 December), p. 24.
        Review of His Toy, His Dream, His Rest.
   It is too early to judge the poem in any
   serious sense, but it is a "dazzling kaleido-
   scope of words," and it may prove to be the
   "complex incomprehensible poem of our complex
   incomprehensible age."

24   JACOBSEN, JOSEPHINE.   Review of His Toy, His
        Dream, His Rest, Baltimore Sunday Sun (17
        November), p. 5D.
        Notes that the volume is "flawed, but
   penetrating," and briefly discusses its
   themes and style.

1968

25   JOHNSON, CAROL. "John Berryman: The Need to
     Exceed," Art International, XII (October),
     21-22.
          From the beginning of his career, Berry-
     man's work has been that of a first-rate
     talent. In the Dream Songs, his most ambi-
     tious work, "technique" takes second place to
     "style," and Berryman tests the boundaries of
     excessiveness by using the "resources of syn-
     tax rather than of language." Reprinted as
     "John Berryman: The Dream Songs," Harvard
     Advocate, CIII (Spring 1969), 23-25 (1969.B32).

26   KESSLER, JASCHA. "The Caged Sybil," SatR, LI
     (14 December), 34-35.
          Review of His Toy, His Dream, His Rest and
     other volumes. Describes Berryman's state-
     ment that he is not Henry as "worthless and
     misleading." Praises the language of the
     poem and Henry's fragmented identity. The
     book is "quite obviously a masterpiece."

27   LASK, THOMAS. "Both In and Out of His Time,"
     New York Times (13 August), p. 37.
          Review of R. W. Stallman's biography of
     Stephen Crane which devotes two paragraphs
     to a description of Berryman's study, noting
     the ingenuity of the Freudian interpretations
     and the style of "this sometimes quirky vol-
     ume."

28   LIEBERMAN, LAURENCE. "The Expansional Poet: A
     Return to Personality," YR, LVII (Winter),
     258-71 [258-62].
          Essay-review of Berryman's Sonnets and
     other works. Berryman, James Dickey and
     William Stafford exemplify the return of per-
     sonality to verse, contra Eliot's dictum

(LIEBERMAN, LAURENCE)
about impersonality. The expansional poet is
not the confessional poet, "limited to writing
autobiography;" rather, he projects "the sum
total of vivid personality" in his work, as
Berryman does in 77 Dream Songs and, to a
lesser extent, in the Sonnets. Very few of
Berryman's sonnets are completely successful,
but when he does succeed, "he is our shrewd-
est clown."

29   MILLS, RALPH J. "Inward Agony and Wonder," Chicago Sun-Times Book Week (3 November), p. 10.
Brief review of His Toy, His Dream, His
Rest, noting the combination of the formal
construction of the songs and the "bold inno-
vation" of their language.

30   MONTAGUE, JOHN. "I Survive You," The Guardian
[Manchester, England] (26 April), p. 7.
Review of Berryman's Sonnets, noting that
the source of Berryman's later style is in
these poems.

31   MORSE, SAMUEL FRENCH. "Twelve Poets," VQR, XLIV
(Summer), 507-12 [510].
Review of Short Poems and other volumes.
Notes the period style of Berryman's early
work and the search for a style that these
poems illustrate.

32   NIGHTENGALE, ERIC. "Professor's Prerogative,"
Skidmore News [Skidmore College] (25 April),
pp. 6-8.
An analysis of Dream Song 14 points out the
success of Berryman's tone. Berryman is "the
best poet in America today": he speaks to
everyone, not just to critics. The Dream
Songs will be as ambitious as Paradise Lost

1968

(NIGHTENGALE, ERIC)
without, as in most long poems, losing in-
tensity as a result of having to include
narrative links.

33   SCHULMAN, GRACE. "Poets and Sonneteers," Shenandoah, XIX (Spring), 73-76.
Review of Berryman's Sonnets and one other
book. Notes the wide range of tone in the
volume and Berryman's ability to make traditional aspects of the sonnet sequence appropriate to a modern work.

34   SEAGER, ALLAN. The Glass House. New York:
McGraw Hill, pp. 158, 206-07, 211, 214, 250.
An account of the part Berryman played, in
Princeton in 1952, in bringing Theodore
Roethke and Edmund Wilson together in a dis-
astrous meeting.

35   SEALY, DOUGLAS. "The Lear of Oklahoma," Irish
Times (11 May).
Review of Berryman's Sonnets. Berryman's
ability to use the sonnet sequence form is
extraordinary: he makes it fit his sensibility so well, it is as if he had invented
the form.

36   SISSON, JONATHAN. "Berryman Reads From New Poems
in N. Y.," Minnesota Daily [University of
Minnesota] (1 November), p. 15.
Brief description of Berryman's reading at
the Hunter College Playhouse on October 25,
1968.

37   SMITH, RAY. "Poetry in Motion: Berryman's 'Toy'
Presents Dialogue of Self and Soul," Minneapolis Star (26 November), p. 2B.

1968

(SMITH, RAY)
   Brief description of His Toy, His Dream,
His Rest, noting the language and some of
the subjects of the "obsessed" and "intense"
poem.

38   STEWART, VINCENT. "Berryman's Sonnets," in
      Masterplots Annual, 1968, edited by Frank N.
      Magill. New York: Salem Press, pp. 28-30.
         Brief discussion of Berryman as confessional
      poet and of the Sonnets, which are seen as a
      revivification of "a fairly tired traditional
      form."

39   SULKEN, RICHARD. "Berryman's Dreams of Death,"
      Columbia Daily Spectator [Columbia University]
      (18 November), p. C3.
         Review of His Toy, His Dream, His Rest.
      Discussion of the central theme of the Dream
      Songs, loss, and a description of the variety
      of Henry's responses to his world. The real
      success of the poem lies in its language and
      in the innovation of the dream song form.

40   SYMONS, JULIAN. "New Poetry," Punch, CCLIV (19
      June), 902.
         Review of Berryman's Sonnets and other vol-
      umes. Compares the volume to Meredith's
      "Modern Love," and praises the Sonnets as
      "subtle" and "delightful."

41   THOMPSON, JOHN. "An Alphabet of Poets," New York
      Review of Books, XI (1 August), 33-36 [34-35].
         Review of Short Poems and other volumes.
      Description of the development of Berryman's
      style, including a brief discussion of the
      language and prosody of "The Lightning,"
      which because of its place in the development

1968

(THOMPSON, JOHN)
of Berryman's verse, is a "key poem in the
history of contemporary verse."

42   THWAITE, ANTHONY. "Guts, Brains, Nerves," New
Statesman, LXXV (17 May), 659.
Review of Berryman's Sonnets and other volumes. Describes the volume as "the quite
awful spasmodics" of Berryman's work.

43   TOLER, SISTER COLETTE. "Strength and Tenderness,"
Spirit, XXXV (November), 149-50.
Review of Homage to Mistress Bradstreet,
concentrating on the tension in the poem between Anne Bradstreet's sensuality and desire
for freedom and her commitment to the harsh
Puritan doctrine.

44   TUBE, HENRY. "Henry's Youth," Spectator, CCXX
(26 April), 566-67.
Review of Berryman's Sonnets. Praises the
language of the sequence, but notes that
Berryman suffers from a "left-over romanti-
cism" which mars them.

45   VENDLER, HELEN. "Savage, Rueful, Irrepressible
Henry," New York Times Book Review (3 November), pp. 1, 58-59.
Review of His Toy, His Dream, His Rest.
Brief description of the development of Berryman's style from the early poems to the Dream
Songs. Notes that this second volume of
dream songs, with its many elegies, is more
mournful than the first. Praises Berryman's
use of "everyday speech."

46   WASSERSTROM, WILLIAM. "Cagey John: Berryman as
Medicine Man," CentR, XII (Summer), 334-54.

(WASSERSTROM, WILLIAM)
An examination of 77 Dream Songs in light
of the epigraphs from Lamentations, Olive
Schreiner and Carl Wittke's Tambo and Bones,
as well as Berryman's biography of Stephen
Crane. Lamentations provides the structure
of the poem, based on numerology, and also
describes the thematic center of the poem:
"fear not." Berryman shares Olive Schreiner's
desire to celebrate the vitality of men despite their maimed condition. The minstrel
show provides clues to the three-part form of
the book, as well as to its style. A comparison of Crane's Henrys and Berryman's
Henry yields insights into the structure of
that character. See also 1970.A1; 1971.B23.

47 WATSON, CATHERINE. "Berryman Ends Poem of 13
        Years," Minneapolis Tribune (12 May), p. 1E.
        Interview with Berryman after his finishing
the Dream Songs. Berryman briefly discusses
the poem, his past career, and his plans for
the future.

1969 A BOOKS

1 MARTZ, WILLIAM J. John Berryman. University of
        Minnesota Pamphlets on American Writers,
        no. 85. Minneapolis: University of Minne-
        sota Press.
        First published monograph on Berryman.
Berryman's poetry is chronologically divided
into two parts, the dividing line being provided by the syntactic shifts of Homage to
Mistress Bradstreet. The Berryman of the
early poetry "offers a subjective response
to the objective reality of the modern world,"
especially the world of World War II, but the

65

1969

(MARTZ, WILLIAM J.)
voice in these poems is too frequently "flat"
and "academic." Berryman's problem is not so
much finding or developing a style as it is
finding "how or to what style is best applied."
In Homage to Mistress Bradstreet, with the
discovery of narrative, Berryman solves that
problem. The Dream Songs is a considerable
achievement, but there is a lack of coherent
structure in the poem--it works by a process
of "cumulative impact" rather than "organic
structure."

1969 B SHORTER WRITINGS

1   ANON. "Berryman, John," Encyclopedia Americana,
        V. 3. International edition. New York:
        Americana Corporation, p. 616.
           Brief entry describing Berryman's career.

2   ANON. "Poetry Was Once Nonsense to Berryman,"
        Minneapolis Tribune (6 January), p. 22.
           Notice of Berryman's sharing the Bollingen
        Prize for His Toy, His Dream, His Rest with
        Karl Shapiro. Brief interview recording his
        responses and stating his plans for the
        future.

3   ANON. "Berryman Receives Award," The Times
        [London] (7 January), p. 4. (6* edition
        only.)

4   ANON. "Poetry: Combatting Society With Sur-
        realism," Time, XCIII (24 January), 72.
           Review of His Toy, His Dream, His Rest,
        noting the use of "the personal voice" in
        recent American poetry and describing the
        Dream Songs as "a major achievement."

1969

5 ANON. "The Book Industry Presents the 20th
        National Book Awards," Publisher's Weekly,
        CXCV (24 March), 26-30 [28-29].
            Notice of Berryman's receiving the National
        Book Award for His Toy, His Dream, His Rest;
        description of the award ceremonies; brief
        excerpts from Berryman's acceptance speech.

6 ANON. "Congested Funeral: Berryman's New Dream
        Songs," TLS, LXVIII (26 June), 680.
            A review of His Toy, His Dream, His Rest
        that examines the Dream Songs as a whole,
        describing the structure (one of accretion),
        "motive" (self-examination of the poet), and
        themes (among others, "the artist's way of
        life in America now"). Reprinted in TLS:
        Essays and Reviews From the Times Literary
        Supplement, 1969. London: Oxford University
        Press, 1970, pp. 134-39.

7 ANON. Review of His Toy, His Dream, His Rest,
        VQR, XLV (Winter), xvi.
            It is too soon to judge the Dream Songs,
        but it doesn't seem to be as good as "we
        dreamed it should be."

8 AIKEN, CONRAD. "A Letter," Harvard Advocate,
        CIII (Spring), 23.
            Brief letter praising His Toy, His Dream,
        His Rest (while noting that the first 77
        Dream Songs weren't completely successful),
        and describing The Dream Songs as "a comic
        strip tease in poetry."

9 ALVAREZ, A. "Berryman's Nunc Dimittis," The
        Observer [London] (4 May), p. 30.
            Review of His Toy, His Dream, His Rest,
        noting that this second installment of dream
        songs "seems better, purer" than the first;

1969

(ALVAREZ, A.)
the many elegies turn the poem into a lament
for an entire generation of American writers.
The poem is obviously autobiographical, but
the style makes Henry not a character existing
in history, but a voice.

10   ANDREWS, LYMAN. "Dream Worlds," The Sunday Times
[London] (1 June), p. 54.
Review of His Toy, His Dream, His Rest.
In the Dream Songs, Berryman imposes "his own
logic" on a disordered world. His achieve-
ment is matched only by Lowell's For the Union
Dead.

11   ATLAS, JAMES. "The Dream Songs: To Terrify and
Comfort," Poetry, CXV (October), 43-46.
Review of His Toy, His Dream, His Rest,
praising its eloquence, describing the terror in the songs, and noting that Henry is
the archetypal modern poet-victim.

12   BORDERS, WILLIAM. "Berryman and Shapiro Share
Award," New York Times (6 January), p. 36.
Notice of Berryman's sharing the Bollingen
Prize with Karl Shapiro, with a brief description of His Toy, His Dream, His Rest. Berryman is quoted as saying that he has "two new
books of poetry 'in preparation.'"

13   BROWNJOHN, ALAN. "Henry Himself," New Statesman,
LXXVII (30 May), 776.
Review of His Toy, His Dream, His Rest and
other volumes. Notes the considerable
achievement of the Dream Songs, but questions
whether major work can result from such intense preoccupation with "the detailed difficulties of living and writing."

14   BURNS, GERALD. "Meditative Verse: Lyric to
         Economic," SWR, LIV (Winter), 91-95 [92].
         Brief note describing His Toy, His Dream,
         His Rest, especially the language of the poem.

15   CONNELLY, KENNETH. "Henry Pussycat, He Come Home
         Good," YR, LVIII (Spring), 419-27.
         Review of His Toy, His Dream, His Rest,
         noting the influence of Joyce: the emphasis
         on the family, Henry's similarities to Bloom
         and Finnegan, the "heavy daughter" as Molly-
         figure. The confusion of pronouns in the
         poem is "the farthest reach of the strategy"
         of Dante: "in this our life, I came to my-
         self."

16   CORRIGAN, ROBERT A. "Ezra Pound and the Bollingen
         Prize," in The Forties: Fiction, Poetry,
         Drama, edited by Warren French. Deland, Fla.:
         Everett/ Edwards, Inc., pp. 287-95.
         An account of Berryman's part in the con-
         troversy surrounding the awarding of the
         Bollingen Prize to Pound for The Pisan Cantos.
         See also 1971.B28.

17   CURLEY, DOROTHY NYREN, ET AL. "Berryman, John,"
         Modern American Literature. 4th edition.
         New York: Frederick Ungar, pp. 101-04.
         Selections from the critical responses to
         Berryman's work from 1941-1961.

18   DAVIS, DOUGLAS M. "Poets Are Finding New Room to
         Stretch Out," National Observer (9 September),
         p. 4B.

19   DICKEY, WILLIAM. "A Place in the Country," HudR,
         XXII (Summer), 347-64 [360-62].
         The language of His Toy, His Dream, His
         Rest is able to deal with a wide range of

1969

(DICKEY, WILLIAM)
experience and creates a world of its own.
The poem is uneven, but "finally impressive
and successful."

20   DODSWORTH, MARTIN. "Henry's Hobble," The Listener, XXII (May), 731.
Review of His Toy, His Dream, His Rest,
noting the thematic import of the conflict
between Henry's sense of responsibility and
his desire for death. The Dream Songs as a
whole "make a new, modern masterpiece."

21   DONOGHUE, DENIS. "Berryman's Long Dream," Art
International, XIII (20 March), 61-64.
The distinctions between Berryman and Henry,
clear in the early dream songs, even when
Berryman is using his own experience, breaks
down in His Toy, His Dream, His Rest. Henry
in pieces, able to identify with all victims,
becomes one voice, Berryman's own, "doctri-
naire, edgy, magisterial." Dream Song 385
analyzed here, in which Berryman intentionally
speaks in his own voice, distinguishing himself from Henry, is an exception.

22   ENGLE, MONROE. "An Educational Incident," Harvard Advocate, CIII (Spring), 18.
Memoir of Berryman at Harvard and Princeton,
describing the environment of the Sonnets
and Berryman's reverence for and knowledge of
the poetry of Gerard Manly Hopkins.

23   EWART, GAVIN. "Making a Language," Ambit, XL
(1969), 44-46.
Praises the "technical control" of His Toy,
His Dream, His Rest, as well as the extraordinary mixture of the comic and the solemn,
the creation of a language and the "grandeur

1969

(EWART, GAVIN)
of design" that make the poem such a memorable
achievement.

24 FITZGERALD, ROBERT. "The Dream Songs," Harvard
        Advocate, CIII (Spring), 24.
            Brief note praising the Dream Songs.

25 GELPI, ALBERT. "Homage to Berryman's Homage,"
        Harvard Advocate, CIII (Spring), 14–17.
            Homage to Mistress Bradstreet is Berryman's
        first masterpiece and the turning point in his
        career. The stanza form and the language are
        perfectly adapted to his theme, the life of
        the poet in America. The poem is not exactly
        an historical poem, since its subject is as
        much Berryman's sensibility and destiny as
        Bradstreet's.

26 GOLDMAN, MICHAEL. "Berryman: Without Impudence
        and Vanity," Nation, CCVIII (24 February),
        245–46.
            Review of His Toy, His Dream, His Rest,
        praising the language of the poem and noting
        that the "narrative framework" of the poem is
        less important than the recurring themes of
        "Death, Fame and Love."

27 GRANT, DAMIAN. "Late Excellence," Tablet (16
        August), 812.
            Praises His Toy, His Dream, His Rest, and
        notes that through his art, Berryman rises
        above the tragic vision that the poem presents.

28 HOLDER, ALAN. "Anne Bradstreet Resurrected," CP,
        II (Spring), 11–18.
            In Homage to Mistress Bradstreet, Berryman
        relies a great deal on Helen Campbell's Anne
        Bradstreet and Her Time. Although Berryman

(HOLDER, ALAN)
sometimes follows the historical facts quite
closely, he occasionally exaggerates, dis-
torts or creates his own 'facts', succumbing
to a "desire to see the past as it should
have been." He does not give us a portrait
of the historical Anne Bradstreet, but creates a memorable figure nevertheless, perhaps
a new "American literary legend."

29 HOLMES, RICHARD. "From Mistress Bradstreet to
    the Boston Sound," The Times [London] (10
    May), p. 21.
        His Toy, His Dream, His Rest is an often
    excellent volume describing Berryman growing
    old amid the deaths of his friends. Berryman,
    "often with exquisite rightness," is the "con-
    fessor to the confessional poets."

30 HONIG, EDWIN. "Berryman's Achievement," Cam-
    bridge Review (30 May), 377-78.
        Review of His Toy, His Dream, His Rest,
    noting that the style is less compact than
    in 77 Dream Songs, and that the poem is more
    impressive in its parts than as a whole.

31 HOWELL, ANTHONY. "A Question of Form," PoetryR,
    LX (Spring), 41-49.
        Essay-review of Berryman's Sonnets that
    distinguishes between classical poetry and
    baroque poetry, the former being one of form
    and meaning, the latter one of novelty and
    decoration. By his successful use of it,
    Shakespeare has defined the sonnet sequence
    as classical; Donne, by his successful use of
    the song, has defined it as baroque. Berry-
    man, as the Dream Songs make clear, is a
    baroque poet; his talents don't fit the

1969

(HOWELL, ANTHONY)
  classical requirements of the sonnet sequence
  form, which explains the failure of the
  Sonnets.

32 JOHNSON, CAROL. "John Berryman: The Dream
      Songs," Harvard Advocate, CIII (Spring), 23–
      25.
        Reprints "John Berryman: The Need to Ex-
      ceed," Art International, XII (October), 21–
      22 (1968.B25), q. v.

33 KAVANAGH, P. J. "A Giving Man," The Guardian
      (8 May), p. 7.

34 LASK, THOMAS. "From One Age, Two Visitors," New
      York Times (6 January), p. 36.
        Comparison of Karl Shapiro's verse and
      Berryman's (occasioned by their sharing the
      Bollingen Prize). Shapiro has been concerned
      principally with moral values; Berryman,
      viewing "the poem as a problem of structure
      and artifact," has made a poetry of personal
      allusion.

35 LINDROTH, JAMES R. Review of His Toy, His Dream,
      His Rest and Lowell's Notebook, 1967–68,
      Spirit, XXXVI (Fall), 36–40.
        Berryman and Lowell share surrealist tech-
      niques and the thematic concerns of "violence,
      sickness and death"; Lowell, however, rejects
      the unity of the sequence, while Berryman
      "creates unity" through the character of
      Henry and his preoccupation with loss.

36 LOWELL, ROBERT. "John Berryman," Harvard Advo-
      cate, CIII (Spring), 17.
        Short note praising the Dream Songs as "the
      single most heroic work" since Pound's Pisan
      Cantos.

37   McCLELLAND, DAVID, ET AL. "An Interview With
        John Berryman," Harvard Advocate, CIII
        (Spring), 4-9.
            The central subject of the interview is the
        Dream Songs: the relation between Henry and
        Berryman, form, language, narrative. Berry-
        man also touches on his past career.

38   MAZZARO, JEROME. "Berryman's Dream World," KR,
        XXXI (Spring), 259-63.
            Review of His Toy, His Dream, His Rest,
        noting the influence of Freud, describing
        "Henry's purpose" as overcoming the sense of
        isolation that followed his fall in Song I,
        and finding numerological and thematic par-
        allels between the Dream Songs and Revela-
        tions.

39   MEREDITH, WILLIAM. "A Bright Surviving Actual
        Scene: Berryman's Sonnets," Harvard Advocate,
        CIII (Spring), 19-22.
            The central conflict in the sequence is be-
        tween Berryman's love and his sense of honor.
        The relation between Berryman's life and his
        art here is similar to the relation in the
        Dream Songs: the poetry serves as an "al-
        chemical solution," turning a "faulty experi-
        ence" into a "faultless reality."

40   MILLS, RALPH J., JR. Creation's Very Self: On
        the Personal Element in Recent American
        Poetry. Fort Worth: Texas Christian Uni-
        versity, pp. 29-32.
            Although Berryman disclaims identity with
        Henry in the Dream Songs, it is clearly
        Berryman's consciousness that we are pre-
        sented with in the poem. The relation be-
        tween Berryman and the speaker of the poem
        can be described best by a line from Song 370:

(MILLS, RALPH J., JR.)
"Naked the man came forth in his mask, to be."
Thus, although the songs are personal, they
move out to the general.

41 MORITZ, CHARLES, ED. "Berryman, John," Current
Biography Yearbook 1969. New York: H. W.
Wilson, pp. 40-42.
Description, based on reviews and articles,
of Berryman's life and work up to 1969.

42 MURPHY, PAT. "'People Individuals With Values':
Poet John Berryman Talks About Life, War,
Death," The State Journal [Lansing, Michigan]
(11 May), p. E9.
Berryman principally discusses his attitudes
towards his students and his thoughts on the
Vietnam War.

43 O'HARA, J. D. "Berryman's Everyman," Chicago
Tribune Book World (7 December), p. 6.
Review of The Dream Songs. The poem's
language is unnatural; the themes of many of
the songs are cliches. The songs are "evoca-
tive" only when Berryman is writing about the
deaths of his friends and other "basic human
events."

44 PARKER, DEREK. "Hats Off--A Genius," PoetryR,
LX (Autumn), 211.
Brief review of The Dream Songs, noting the
obscurity of some of the songs, but praising
the whole as "a masterpiece."

45 PEARSON, GABRIEL. "John Berryman," in The Modern
Poet, edited by Ian Hamilton. New York:
Horizon Press, pp. 111-24.
Reprint of "John Berryman--Poet as Medium,"
The Review, XV (April, 1965), 3-17 (1965.B29),
q. v.

46   PEROSA, SERGIO. "Prefazione" and "Note," Omaggio
         a Mistress Bradstreet. Torino: Giulio
         Einaudi Editore, pp. 5-18, 81-95.
            The preface and notes to the Italian trans-
         lation of Homage to Mistress Bradstreet.

47   RAYMONT, HENRY. "National Book Awards; The Win-
         ners," New York Times (11 March), p. 42.
            Notice of Berryman's receiving the National
         Book Award for His Toy, His Dream, His Rest.
         See also 1969.B52.

48   RICH, ADRIENNE. "Living With Henry," Harvard
         Advocate, CIII (Spring), 10-11.
            The Dream Songs go beyond literature to
         poetry, "and poetry is life." Berryman is
         seriously concerned with moral questions; his
         language is our American amalgam. His Toy,
         His Dream, His Rest, more open and freer than
         77 Dream Songs, is "a poem of victory" of
         life and love over death.

49   SEYMOUR-SMITH, MARTIN. "Bones Dreams On," Spec-
         tator, CCXXII (9 May), 622-23.
            Review of His Toy, His Dream, His Rest.
         Notes that Berryman's interest in technique
         has not changed throughout his career, but
         that in the Dream Songs Berryman is trying to
         rid himself of "false coherence" inappropriate
         to the period. Although some of the songs are
         "impenetrable," the volume as a whole is "pro-
         foundly liberating."

50   SHAPIRO, KARL. "Major Poets of the Ex-English
         Language," Washington Post Book World (26
         January), p. 4.
            Review of His Toy, His Dream, His Rest and
         one other volume. Describes Berryman's songs
         as elegies and praises the language highly.

51   SHEEHAN, DONALD. "Varieties of Technique: Some
        Recent Books of American Poetry," CL, X
        (Spring), 284-302 [287-90].
            Review of Berryman's Sonnets and other works.
        Describes the sequence and compares it to the
        Dream Songs.

52   SHERMAN, JOHN K. "Berryman Wins $1,000 for
        Poetry," Minneapolis Star (11 March), p. 22B.
            Notice of Berryman's winning the National
        Book Award for His Toy, His Dream, His Rest.
        See also 1969.B47.

53   TAYLOR, HENRY. "His Toy, His Dream, His Rest,"
        in Masterplots Annual, 1969, edited by Frank
        N. Magill. New York: Salem Press, pp. 152-
        56.
            Discussion of some central aspects of the
        Dream Songs--the theme of loss and the rela-
        tion of Berryman to Henry--with the realiza-
        tion that the poem raises many questions that
        will only be answered after years of critical
        examination.

54   TOKUNAGA, SHOZO. "Yume no Henkyo wo yuko John
        Berryman" ["Berryman's Journey Through the
        Dreamland"], EigoS, CXV (October), 616-18.

55   TULIP, JAMES. "The American Dream of John Berry-
        man," Poetry Australia, no. 31 (December),
        45-48.
            Review of The Dream Songs, noting the simi-
        larities in form between In Memoriam and
        Berryman's poem, and the differences between
        them in thematic attitudes. The poem is uni-
        fied by Berryman's "intelligence, feeling and
        wit," more successfully so in the first 77
        than in His Toy, His Dream, His Rest.

1969

56 TURNER, WILLIAM PRICE. "The Wild and the Wilder-
       ness," Twentieth Century, CLXXVII, 45-46.
          Review of His Toy, His Dream, His Rest and
       one other volume. The word-play in the poem
       is "self-indulgent" and "tiresome." The best
       work in the volume is to be found in the songs
       mourning Delmore Schwartz's death.

57 VAN DOREN, MARK. "John Berryman," Harvard Advo-
       cate, CIII (Spring), 17.
          Brief note describing Berryman as a student
       at Columbia and praising his art.

58 WALSH, MALACHY. "John Berryman: A Novel Inter-
       pretation," Viewpoint [Georgetown University],
       X (Spring), 5-21.
          Explication of five dream songs (78, 125,
       247, 305, 385) by way of showing that The
       Dream Songs works like a psychological novel,
       the theme of which is Henry's attempt to re-
       create himself from a minimalized Cartesian
       consciousness ("eyeteeth & a block of memo-
       ries").

1970 A BOOKS

1 BERNDT, SUSAN G. "The Dream Songs of John Berry-
       man." Master's thesis, East Tennessee State
       University.
          An examination of The Dream Songs in light
       of the four epigraphs to 77 Dream Songs. The
       first epigraph directs us to the "crisis of
       faith in the face of suffering" that is the
       subject of the poem. The second establishes
       the minstrel form of dialogue between the two
       end men and sets the tone. The third indicates
       a possible source for Berryman's prosody in
       the Hebrew funeral songs. The fourth presents

(BERNDT, SUSAN G.)
　　the metaphysical and philosophical content of
　　the poem as well as the dream method.

2　BRENNER, PATRICIA ANN. "John Berryman's Dream
　　Songs: Manner and Matter." Ph.D. disserta-
　　tion, Kent State University.
　　　The Dream Songs is influenced principally
　　by Whitman, Hegel and Freud. It is an epic
　　narrative that describes three main odysseys:
　　a journey to the past, Henry's birth as a
　　being and a poet and a final integration that
　　allows Henry to view the world realistically.
　　Each of the odysseys is associated with a
　　Hegelian and a Freudian element: thesis,
　　antithesis, synthesis of Hegelian logic; id,
　　ego and a combination of the two of Freudian
　　psychology.

1970 B　SHORTER WRITINGS

1　ANON. Review of The Dream Songs, VQR, XLVI
　　(Spring), xlivi.
　　　Brief note, describing the poem.

2　ANON. Review of The Dream Songs, Choice, VII
　　(June), 539.
　　　Brief review, noting some of the differences
　　between the Henry of 77 Dream Songs and the
　　Henry of His Toy, His Dream, His Rest (Henry
　　is more the "professor-poet" in the latter
　　volume).

3　ANON. Review of Love & Fame, Kirkus Reviews,
　　XXXVIII (15 September), 1065.
　　　The first two sections of the book are not
　　particularly rewarding, but the hospital se-
　　quence and the "Eleven Addresses to the Lord"
　　more than make up for this.

4   ANON. "News Notes," Poetry, CXVII (November), 127.
    Note that Berryman was one of the judges
    for the Delmore Schwartz Memorial Poetry
    Award.

5   BERG, MARTIN. "A Truly Gentle Man Tightens and
    Paces: An Interview With John Berryman,"
    Minnesota Daily [University of Minnesota]
    (20 January), pp. 9, 10, 14, 15, 17.
    In this interview, which dates roughly from
    the time of the publication of Love & Fame,
    Berryman discusses, among other things,
    Frost, Love & Fame, and simplicity and "trans-
    parency" in high art.

6   BLY, ROBERT. "A Garage Sale of Berryman's Po-
    etry," Minneapolis Tribune (13 December), pp.
    10E-11E.
    Review of The Dream Songs, which are de-
    scribed as "utter drivel." Berryman is
    simply a "boring academic poet," clearing out
    the "useless details" of thirty years of
    teaching into this "garage sale" of poetry.

7   BURNS, GERALD. "Innocent Serpents and a Cunning
    Dove," SWR, LV (Winter), 96-99 [97-98].
    Review of Berryman's Sonnets and The Dream
    Songs as well as other books. Notes that the
    moral dilemma is more important to Berryman
    in the Sonnets than the literary dilemma.
    Praises the language of The Dream Songs, but
    notes that the suffering described in the
    volume is not convincing.

8   CARRUTH, HAYDEN. "Love, Art and Money," Nation,
    CCXI (2 November), 437-38.
    Review of Love & Fame which also discusses
    Berryman's career as a whole. Berryman's
    fame is inflated--he is a more minor poet

1970

(CARRUTH, HAYDEN)

than many of his peers. The quotation from
R. P. Blackmur in "Olympus" points out one
of the ways in which Berryman went wrong as
a poet--by interpreting Blackmur's "fresh
idiom" to mean "twisted and posed language."
Berryman replied to this review in a letter
printed in the Nation, CCXI (30 November),
546, claiming that Carruth had misread his
verse.

9   COOPER, PHILIP. The Autobiographical Myth of
        Robert Lowell. Chapel Hill: University of
        North Carolina Press, pp. 141-43.
            Briefly discusses The Dream Songs as "one
        of the most immediate antecedents" of Lowell's
        Notebook.

10 CUSHMAN, JEROME. Review of Love & Fame, LJ,
        LXIII (1 December), 4180.
            Brief description of the book, noting Berry-
        man's good humor and the Rabelaisian aspects
        of the poetry.

11 DODSWORTH, MARTIN. "John Berryman: An Intro-
        duction," The Survival of Poetry. London:
        Faber and Faber, pp. 100-32.
            Berryman's verse appears to be an extension
        of the modernist tradition, rooted in the work
        of the Symbolists: it is highly allusive,
        conducive to conventional explication, and
        self-consciously "Literary." But Berryman's
        intent, especially in The Dream Songs, is to
        undermine the notion that poetry is something
        apart from the real world. By the "super-
        fluous oddity of his style" and the excessive
        emotions in The Dream Songs, Berryman is in-
        sisting that his poetry is, as he described
        Stephen Crane's, "said for use." The Dream

1970

(DODSWORTH, MARTIN)
   Songs are thus a record of "the painful
   process of an acceptance of the way the world
   is" and constitute a direct "attack on a
   stultifying notion of Literature."

12   ESHELMAN, CLAYTON. Review of His Toy, His Dream,
     His Rest, MinnR, X (January–April), 79–80.
        Berryman's hiding his madness behind a per-
     sona is irritating; the language of the poem
     is "toneless, dead."

13   FINK, GUIDO. "Ribellioni Rientrate: Berryman/
     Bradstreet," Paragone, XXI (1970), 125–31.

14   FULLER, EDMUND. "Poetry of Two Unusual Men:
     Frost and Berryman," Wall Street Journal (12
     January), p. 12.
        Review of The Dream Songs and The Poetry of
     Robert Frost. Describes the poem, noting
     that Berryman solves the "problem" of the
     long poem by arranging the songs as a "loose
     chronicle" of Henry's inner and outer life.

15   HAYES, ANN L. "The Voices of John Berryman,"
     International Poetry Forum (Pittsburgh).
        Berryman transforms his personal experiences
     and emotions into poetry by adopting different
     voices: the voice of Anne Bradstreet, the
     "direct first person" of the Sonnets, the
     "voice of the self in dreams" of Henry, who
     combines the advantages of both the personal
     and the fictive voices. Reprinted in John
     Berryman Studies, I (July), 17–20 (1975.B7).

16   HAYMAN, RONALD. "The City and the House," En-
     counter, XXIV (February), 84–91 [86–87].
        Review of His Toy, His Dream, His Rest and
     other books. Despite individually successful

82

(HAYMAN, RONALD)
   songs, the Dream Songs is a failure. Henry's
   surname (House) represents a withdrawal from
   Williams' identification of the poet with the
   city, but too often that withdrawal is into
   merely trivial personal matters.

17   HEYEN, WILLIAM. "Fourteen Poets: A Chronicle,"
      SoR, VI (Spring), 539-50 [546-47].
         Short note on Berryman's Sonnets, calling
      it a "brilliant performance."

18   HOFFMAN, DANIEL. "John Berryman," in Contemporary
      Poets of the English Language, edited by
      Rosalie Murphy. Chicago: St. James Press,
      pp. 85-87.
         Brief biographical and bibliographical
      entry and discussion of the Sonnets, Homage
      to Mistress Bradstreet and The Dream Songs.

19   KOSTELANETZ, RICHARD. "Conversation With Berry-
      man," MR, XI (Spring), 340-47.
         Berryman is interviewed after winning the
      National Book Award for His Toy, His Dream,
      His Rest. He discusses his career (especially
      the early years) in some detail, and notes the
      tendency in his work to "regard the individual
      soul under stress."

20   MOLESWORTH, CHARLES. "Full Count," Nation, CCX
      (23 February), 217-19.
         Review of The Dream Songs, noting that the
      last third of the book is the weakest, as the
      subject turns more frequently to the writing
      of the songs themselves, but that despite its
      failings, The Dream Songs is "monumental."

21   OBERG, ARTHUR. "John Berryman: The Dream Songs
      and the Horror of Unlove," UWR, VI (Fall),
      1-11.

(OBERG, ARTHUR)
    Despite the many attempts at "distancing"
in The Dream Songs, at the center of the poem
lies "what defines man . . . his capacity for
language and love." The songs are essentially
love songs which recognize the overwhelming
need for and sad lack of caring in the world.

22 RICKS, CHRISTOPHER. "Recent American Poetry,"
        MR, XI (Spring), 313-38 [313-15, 333-38].
        Omnibus review of His Toy, His Dream, His
    Rest and other volumes. Persuasively com-
    pares The Dream Songs with In Memoriam,
    pointing out the similarities in structure
    and theme: they are both long poems made up
    of short lyrics, both elegiac, both theodi-
    cies.

23 SPEARS, MONROE. Dionysus and the City. New York:
        Oxford University Press, pp. 239, 247-50.
        Berryman's attempts to write long poems
    must be judged to be failures--in neither The
    Dream Songs nor Homage to Mistress Bradstreet
    did he find any "satisfactory principle of
    order."

1971 A BOOKS

1   ARPIN, GARY QUINTIN. "The Poetry of John Berry-
        man." Ph.D. dissertation, University of
        Virginia.
        Chronological study of Berryman's verse
    from the early poems through The Dream Songs.
    Berryman's early verse presents the sensi-
    bility of the poet with the moral and physi-
    cal chaos of the Second World War. The poet's
    alternative to this world is found in his
    emphasis on love and work, the two bases of

(ARPIN, GARY QUINTIN)
Freud's (and Berryman's) ideal communities.
In <u>Berryman's Sonnets</u>, Berryman is concerned
with the moral consequences of an act which
violates the laws of the culture as well as
his own commitment to the principles of love
and work. In <u>Homage to Mistress Bradstreet</u>,
Berryman is interested in Anne Bradstreet
principally as a woman faced with the difficulty of living well in a hostile environment.
In <u>The Dream Songs</u>, Henry, like Mistress Bradstreet, finds himself in a pattern of rebellion and acceptance, a pattern completed
by the last two poems. As the poem progresses,
Henry gradually discovers, as all of Berryman's characters have, the importance of love
and work as a means of dealing with the world.

2   FOLLIET, MARY CAROL HANSON. "Poet in the Post-
        Literate Age." Master's thesis, State Uni-
        versity of New York at Stony Brook.
            In an age in which the growth of electronic
        media threatens the printed word, "the revi-
        talization of language will continue to rest
        in the hands of the poets." <u>The Dream Songs</u>
        indicates the way in which this will be
        achieved: redeeming the language, trans-
        forming cliche and colloquialism into the
        stuff of poetry, going beyond traditional
        grammar and syntax and creating "a language
        which transforms the vulgar into the divine."

<u>1971 B   SHORTER WRITINGS</u>

1   ANON. Review of <u>Love & Fame</u>, <u>Booklist</u>, LXVII
        (15 May), 770.
            Brief note describing the book.

1971

2 ANON. "Poetry," New York Times Book Review (6
    June), p. 36.
        Brief note describing Love & Fame. Re-
    printed 5 December, 1971, p. 86.

3 ANON. "Kudos," Time, XCVII (7 June), 35.
        Notice of Berryman's receiving an honorary
    D.Let. from Drake University.

4 ANON. Review of Love & Fame, VQR, XLVII (Autumn),
    clxi, clxiv.
        Notes the new direction that Love & Fame
    represents, and the humor of the book.

5 ANON. "No Shortage of Satisfactions," TLS, LXX
    (24 December), 1602.
        Review of Love & Fame and other volumes.
    Notes that the subjects of many of the poems
    are trivial but that the sensationalism and
    the gossip keep one's interest. The poems
    about God, coming after all of the other pre-
    occupations, seem "hardly edifying."

6 BROWNJOHN, ALAN. "Variations," New Statesman,
    LXXXII (24 December), 899-900.
        Love & Fame is not a successful step forward
    from The Dream Songs; the religious resolution
    in Part IV is "disappointing," and the volume
    itself barely "short of boring."

7 BURNS, GERALD. "What to Make of an Unfinished
    Thing," SWR, LVI (Spring), 207-11 [207].
        Review of Love & Fame and other volumes.
    Describes the book, noting that it is "good
    plain verse," but the experiences recounted
    are more impressive than the language used to
    describe them.

8   DALE, PETER. "Slithy Tome," Agenda, IX (Winter),
         52-61.
         Most of the syntactic oddities of The Dream
         Songs do not have any poetic point--they seem
         principally to serve as a substitute for
         structure, giving the reader a sense of a
         world. Berryman's assumption that he is
         writing a major work is necessary to the
         poem--no one would want to read a "long-
         winded account of the creation of a flop"--
         but it is not borne out by the reading. De-
         spite the "almost doctrinaire" reception by
         the critics, The Dream Songs consists of
         "hackneyed subject matter" inflated and dis-
         guised by "bogus" stylistic devices and the
         "artificially imposed prestige of a 'major'
         work."

9   DICKEY, JAMES. Sorties. New York: Doubleday,
         pp. 52, 66, 85, 101.
         A re-evaluation of Dickey's earlier high
         estimation of Berryman's verse (See 1965.B18;
         1968.B16). Berryman's verse is "so phony and
         ersatz" that it has no interest. The proper
         direction for poetry is away from artifice,
         not toward it.

10   FIELD, J. C. "The Literary Scene: 1968-1970,"
         Revue des Langues Vivantes, XXXVII (no. 6),
         766-73 [771-72].
         Praises the language of His Toy, His Dream,
         His Rest, but notes that many of the most im-
         pressive songs are "simpler" and "more ex-
         plicit" than the rest.

11   FRASER, G. S. "The Magicians," PR, XXXVIII (Win-
         ter), 469-78 [470-71].
         Love & Fame is at the same time serious and
         comic; the anecdotes in the book are

1971

(FRASER, G. S.)
reminiscent of Thurber's My Life and Hard
Times. (Letters and rejoinder mentioning
Berryman are printed in PR, XXXIX (Summer,
1972), 471-73.)

12 FUSSELL, PAUL JR. "A Poetic Trip Through
Puberty and Beyond," Los Angeles Times Book
Review (28 February), p. 8.
In Love & Fame, Berryman, finally finished
with Henry, has created an honest and charming
idiom that goes beyond the "exploitation of
confession."

13 HAAS, JOSEPH. "Who Killed Henry Pussycat? I
Did, Says John Berryman, With Love & a Poem,
& for Freedom O," Chicago Daily News Panorama
(6-7 February), pp. 4-5.
Interview with Berryman concentrating on
The Dream Songs, especially the relation between Berryman and Henry. Most of the interview covers material covered in other interviews.

14 HOWES, VICTOR. "On Meeting Mr. John Berryman,
Poet," Christian Science Monitor (18 February),
p. 5.
Love & Fame is Berryman's most personal
book, and one which skirts triviality at
times. But the "Eleven Addresses to the
Lord" may indicate a new direction.

15 JAFFE, DANIEL. "A Sacred Language in the Poet's
Tongue," SatR, LIV (3 April), 31-33, 46 [31].
Love & Fame reveals a great deal of personal
detail, but during the course of the book "the
personal becomes the universal."

16   LEOPOLD, VIVIAN. "He Left a Note," The Review,
       XXVII/XXVIII (Autumn-Winter), 77–79.
          The first half of Love & Fame is reminiscent
       of Making It, but it has a certain amount of
       anecdotal intensity. In the second half,
       Berryman is intense when he writes about him-
       self, "tendentious" when he writes about his
       fellow patients.

17   MAZZARO, JEROME. "False Confessions," Shenandoah,
       XXII (Winter), 86–88.
          Review of Love & Fame. Compares the volume
       to Augustine's Confessions, noting several
       points of similarity. However, Berryman is
       prey to the "imitative fallacy, depicting
       callowness by being callow," and the volume
       is ultimately insincere.

18   MEINERS, R. K. "The Way Out: The Poetry of Del-
       more Schwartz and Others," SoR, VII (Winter),
       314–337 [317–18].
          Omnibus review of Short Poems and other
       volumes. Notes the similarities to be found
       in the early work of Berryman, Lowell and
       Schwartz.

19   MORAMARCO, FRED. "A Gathering of Poets," WHR,
       XXV (Summer), 278–83 [283].
          Review of Love & Fame and other volumes.
       Notes and praises Berryman's new style.

20   MORSE, SAMUEL FRENCH. "Books," Michigan Quarterly,
       X (Fall), 291–95 [291–92].
          Review of Love & Fame and other books. For
       those who don't have private knowledge of
       Berryman's life, most of the book will seem
       "self-indulgent arrogance."

1971

21 MOTTRAM, ERIC. "John Berryman," in The Penguin
    Companion to American Literature, edited by
    Malcolm Bradbury, et al. New York: McGraw-
    Hill, p. 33.
        Brief entry describing Berryman's career
    through 1968.

22 NAIDEN, JAMES. "Poet Notes His 'Love Losses' in
    New Work," Minneapolis Star (12 January),
    p. 2B.
        Love & Fame is a "landmark because of
    Berryman's resurgent powers." He deals with
    his own past and the tragedies of the day in
    a wittier and more meaningful manner than his
    peers. "Eleven Addresses to the Lord" is the
    weakest section of the book. Love & Fame is
    an example of what a first-rate poet can do
    "if he sets his creative powers to the fore."

23 PATRICK, W. B. "Berryman's 77 Dream Songs:
    'Spare Now a Cagey John/A Whilom," SHR, V
    (Spring), 113-19.
        A study of 77 Dream Songs in light of the
    epigraphs and Berryman's biography of Stephen
    Crane, noting Berryman's use of the minstrel
    show and his identification with the suffering
    figures in Lamentations and the work of Olive
    Schreiner. See also 1968.B46; 1971.A1.

24 PHILLIPS, ROBERT. "Balling the Muse," North
    American Review, CCLVII (Winter), 72-73.
        Reprinted as part of "John Berryman's
    Literary Offenses," The Confessional Poets.
    Carbondale and Edwardsville: Southern Illi-
    nois University Press, 1973 (1973.B59), q. v.

25 PRITCHARD, WILLIAM. "Love and Fame," New York
    Times Book Review (24 January), pp. 5, 25.

1971

(PRITCHARD, WILLIAM)
 Berryman's new style is "immensely readable,"
but although the gossip in the book is interesting, it is difficult to sympathize with
Berryman's ego centrism.

26 SAWAZAKI, JUNNOSUKE. "John Berryman no Shiho"
 ["The Poetic Technique of John Berryman"],
 EigoS, CXVI (March), 868-69.

27 SHEEHAN, DONALD. "The Silver Sensibility: Five
 Recent Books of American Poetry," CL, XII
 (Winter), 98-121 [114-20].
  Omnibus review of His Toy, His Dream, His
 Rest and other volumes. Describes The Dream
 Songs as a late projectivist work. Its mode
 is not autobiographical but musical: at its
 center stands "the Singer" and the poem is
 about whatever "the Singer" sings. The problem with the form is that it can properly
 end only with the death of "the Singer," and
 although Henry does die near the end of the
 poem, he returns. Thus Berryman has let himself in for the same fate as Pound: "the
 poem that refuses to let go."

28 SQUIRES, RADCLIFFE. Allen Tate. New York: Bobbs
 Merrill, pp. 122, 186-88, 213.
  Describes Berryman's part in the controversy
 following the award of the Bollingen Prize to
 Ezra Pound for the Pisan Cantos. See also
 1969.B16.

29 VONALT, LARRY P. "Berryman's The Dream Songs,"
 SR, LXXIX (Summer), 464-69.
  A brief, but comprehensive and persuasive
 discussion of the poem, touching on its central themes and methods, and noting its religious dimension.

John Berryman: A Reference Guide

1972 A BOOKS

1 KELLY, RICHARD. <u>John Berryman: A Checklist</u>.
   Metuchen, New Jersey: The Scarecrow Press.
   Contains a chronology and a list of Berryman's works divided into the following categories: books, contributions to books, articles and reviews in periodicals, uncollected
   poems in periodicals and annuals, selected anthologies containing Berryman's poems, short
   stories, recordings. Also contains a list of
   works about Berryman, divided into the following categories: reviews, biographical
   articles, interviews, general critiques, mono-
   graphs, and indexes. The preface contains
   a brief memoir of Berryman as a teacher in
   addition to the customary prefatory material.
   For descriptions of the forward and introduc-
   tion ("In Loving Memory of the Late Author
   of 'The Dream Songs'" and "The Epistemology
   of Loss"), <u>see</u> 1972.B58 and 1972.B24.

1972 B SHORTER WRITINGS

1 ANON. "Poet Berryman Leaps to Death," Saint Paul
   <u>Dispatch</u> (7 January), pp. 1, 2.
   Obituary and description of Berryman's
   suicide.

2 ANON. "John Berryman, American Poet," <u>The Times</u>
   [London] (8 January), p. 16.
   Berryman's work deserves to be called
   "metaphysical" for its "dense mixture of in-
   tellectuality and physicality."

3 ANON. "John Berryman, Leading U. S. Poet, Jumps
   to Death," <u>The Times</u> [London] (8 January),
   p. 1.
   Notice of Berryman's suicide.

4   ANON. "John Berryman, Poet, Is Dead; Won the
        Pulitzer Prize in 1965," <u>New York Times</u>
        (8 January), p. 33.
            Notice of Berryman's suicide.

5   ANON. "Poet Berryman Killed in Plunge From
        Bridge," Minneapolis <u>Tribune</u> (8 January),
        pp. 1A, 3A.
            Obituary and description of Berryman's
        suicide, including an eye-witness account
        which states that "he never looked back at
        all."

6   ANON. "All We Fall Down & Die . . . ," <u>Minnesota
        Daily</u> [University of Minnesota] (10 January),
        p. 3.
            Comments on Berryman by friends, students
        and colleagues. His sensitivity to suffering
        is especially noted.

7   ANON. "Catholic Rites Set in Berryman Burial,"
        Minneapolis <u>Star</u> (10 January), p. 12B.
            Because of "greater understanding of the
        factors involved in death," Berryman, although
        a suicide, was given Catholic services.

8   ANON. "Letter From Home," Minneapolis <u>Star</u>
        (10 January), p. 12A.
            Berryman, who recently committed suicide,
        was to have participated "on a panel concerned
        with how to cope with death."

9   ANON. "What's News," <u>Wall Street Journal</u> (10
        January), p. 1.
            Brief note regarding Berryman's suicide and
        funeral services.

10 ANON. "Milestones," <u>Time</u>, XCIX (17 January), 53.
            Brief obituary notice.

1972

11   ANON. "Transition," Newsweek, LXXIX (17 January),
         51.
             Brief obituary.

12   ANON. "Obituary Notes," Publisher's Weekly, CCI
         (24 January), 42.
             Brief obituary, giving a short description
         of Berryman's career.

13   ANON. Review of Delusions, Etc., AR, XXXII
         (Spring-Summer), 241-42.
             Brief review, noting the saving aspects of
         Berryman's humor.

14   ANON. Review of Delusions, Etc., Booklist,
         LXVIII (15 July), 965.
             Brief review.

15   ANON. Review of Delusions, Etc., VQR, XLVIII
         (Autumn), cxxi, cxxiv.
             Notes the major themes, the triumph of lan-
         guage and the "implicit sonata form" which
         make the book a coherent whole instead of a
         mere collection.

16   ANON. Review of Delusions, Etc., Choice, IX
         (November), 1126.
             Brief review, noting the richness of Berry-
         man's late style.

17   ANON. "Poetry," SatR, LV (December), 84.
             Brief note on Delusions, Etc.

18   ALVAREZ, A. "I Don't Think I Will Sing Any More,"
         New York Times Book Review (25 June), pp. 1,
         12, 14.
             Review of Delusions, Etc. Berryman's re-
         ligious verse is unconvincing; it seems to be
         a "defence against the appalling sadness"

(ALVAREZ, A.)
   which Berryman saw around him and which per-
   meates Delusions, Etc. Berryman's real subject is grief, as the middle of this book
   shows.

19   . The Savage God: A Study of Suicide. New
        York: Random House, pp. 259-60.
        The Dream Songs began as a "quirky private
        journal," but turned into a long lament for
        the deaths of Berryman's father and his
        friends and ended with an "acceptance of his
        own mortality."

20   AXELROD, STEVEN.   "Colonel Shaw in American Po-
        etry: 'For the Union Dead' and Its Prede-
        cessors," AQ, XXIV (October), 523-37.
        Discussion of four poems about Colonel Shaw
        (including Berryman's "Boston Common") which,
        taken together, "comprise a sort of spiritual
        history of the American intellect." Berry-
        man's poem, which is based largely on William
        James's dedicatory speech, contrasts the her-
        oism of the past with the lack of that capa-
        city among "the dispossessed" of the present.
        See also 1957.B9.

21   BARBERA, JACK. "John Berryman: R.I.P.," JML, II
        (November), 547-53.
        Berryman's father's suicide was at the cen-
        ter of his loss of faith, his own suicidal
        impulses and his great need for love.

22   BAYLEY, JOHN. "Confidences," The Listener (28
        December), 901-02.
        Delusions, Etc. is "disappointing" because
        in a collection of short poems Berryman
        doesn't have the opportunity, as he did in

95

1972

(BAYLEY, JOHN)
The Dream Songs, to build up his "imperial
sway."

23   BERGERSON, ROGER. "Father's Suicide 'Haunted'
Berryman," Saint Paul Pioneer Press (8 January), p. 1.
Obituary, with comments by friends and colleagues on Berryman's death.

24   BERRYHILL, MICHAEL. "The Epistemology of Loss,"
in Richard Kelly, John Berryman: A Checklist.
Metuchen, New Jersey: Scarecrow Press, 1972,
pp. xxi-xxxi (1972.A1).
A brief survey of Berryman's use of allusion
and language, and his basic themes.

25   _____. "'Let Us Listen to Berryman's Music,'"
Minneapolis Sunday Tribune (9 July),
pp. 8D-9D.
Review of Delusions, Etc., noting that although it is tempting to read these poems as
some kind of prediction of Berryman's suicide,
most of them are concerned with Berryman's
religious faith, and some of the 'pessimistic'
poems, such as "Henry's Understanding," actually date from an earlier period.

26   BRENNER, PATRICIA. "John Berryman Is Resting,"
Café Solo, no. 4 (Fall), 14-15.
Memoir of Berryman at Breadloaf in 1962 and
in Minneapolis in 1969.

27   BRESLIN, JOHN B. "A Prospect of Books," America,
CXXVII (7 October), 265-69 [268].
Discussion of books to be published, among
them Recovery, "the final poems [sic] of the
late John Berryman."

28 BURNS, GERALD. "Last Words From Late Poets,"
      SWR, LVII (Summer), 255-56.
        Review of Delusions, Etc. and one other
      volume. Berryman's long poems are more suc-
      cessful than these short ones, although the
      first section, "Opus Dei," is "worth the rest."

29 CALLAHAN, PATRICK J. "Current Books of Poetry,"
      Poet Lore, LXVII (Autumn), 285-89.
        Review of Love & Fame and other volumes.
      The first two parts of the book are of "lit-
      tle interest," but the third and fourth sec-
      tions are quite moving, although it is hard
      to tell if it is the poetry or Berryman's
      confessions that affect the reader.

30 CARDOZO, ARLENE ROSSEN. "John Berryman: Unfor-
      gettable Teacher," Chicago Sun-Times Showcase
      (Book Week) (21 May), p. 2.
        Memoir of Berryman's teaching "Humanities
      in the Modern World" at the University of
      Minnesota in the 1950's, by one of his stu-
      dents of that time.

31 CIARDI, JOHN. "Note," SatR, LV (20 May), 48.
        Brief description of Berryman's career and
      his suicide.

32 CLEMONS, WALTER. "Man on a Tightrope," Newsweek,
      LXXIX (1 May), 113-14.
        Review of Delusions, Etc. Brief description
      of Berryman's career. Notes the "sober style"
      of Berryman's last poems.

33 CLOSE, ROY M. "Death Was a Recurring Theme in
      Life Work of Poet Berryman," Minneapolis Star
      (8 January), p. 15A.
        Obituary, noting the preoccupation with
      death in Berryman's work. Description of

1972

(CLOSE, ROY M.)
  Berryman as a teacher; comments by friends
  and colleagues.

34 _____. "Berryman's Last Poems Reflect His Relationship With Subjects," Minneapolis Star
  (11 May), p. 5B.

35 COOK, BRUCE. "Berryman, 1914-1972: 'I Am Headed
  West Also,'" National Observer (22 January),
  p. 21.
    Memoir of Berryman's giving a reading in
  Chicago several years before. Description of
  his recent poetry as "suicide notes."

36 DALE, PETER. "Three Poets: Can Belief and Form
  Come in Bags of Tricks?" SatR, LV (8 July),
  57-58.
    The answer to the question posed by the
  title is, for Berryman's work, no. Berryman
  cannot indulge his belief because he relies
  on mannerism rather than a "personal sense of
  rhythm or form," and because his career has
  not led us to expect belief from him. As a
  result, the poems in Delusions, Etc. are weak
  and unconvincing, with stylistic "gimmicks"
  covering a "thinness of thought."

37 DAY, STACEY B. Review of Delusions, Etc., Bulle-
  tin of the Bell Museum of Pathology [Univer-
  sity of Minnesota], I (Autumn), 32-33.
    A stream-of-consciousness review, cele-
  brating Berryman's kindness, sensitivity and
  ability with language. Delusions, Etc. is
  "not a book of delusions. This is a book of
  Realities."

JOHN BERRYMAN: A REFERENCE GUIDE

38 DORBIN, SANDY. "Vision and Craft, Humor and Suf-
        fering," LJ, XCVII (15 April), 1441.
            Brief review of Delusions, Etc., describing
        Berryman as "nearly a giant."

39 DUFFY, MARTHA. "The Last Prayers," Time, XCIX
        (1 May), 81.
            Briefly compares Berryman's work with Sylvia
        Plath's, and notes that in Delusions, Etc.
        Berryman had reached a psychological end-
        point: "the realization that for him nothing
        was going to work."

40 DUNN, DOUGLAS. "A Bridge in Minneapolis," En-
        counter, XXXVIII (May), 73-78 [73-74].
            Review of Love & Fame, noting the irony im-
        plicit in the structure, each section "can-
        cel[ling] out its predecessor."

41 EPSTEIN, HENRIETTA. "John Berryman Is Dead," The
        South End (12 January).

42 HARSENT, DAVID. "Poetae Sepulchrum," Spectator,
        CCXXVIII (12 February), 238.
            Review of Love and Fame and other volumes.
        The lack of an inventive, dream song style
        reduces some of the reminiscences in this
        book to the trivial.

43 HARTGEN, STEPHEN. "Pulitzer Poet Berryman Jumps
        Off Bridge to Death," Minneapolis Star (7 Jan-
        uary), pp. 1-2.
            Obituary and description of Berryman's sui-
        cide.

44   HAZO, SAMUEL. "The Death of John Berryman," Com-
         monweal, XCV (25 February), 489–90.
            Memoir of Berryman reading at the Inter-
         national Poetry Forum in Pittsburgh and a
         view of the last section of Love & Fame as a
         preparation for his death.

45   HOWES, VICTOR. "'Into the Terrible Water,'"
         Christian Science Monitor (31 May), p. 11.
            Delusions, Etc. is an "openhearted, humorous"
         portrait of a very troubled man. Its style
         and imagery contain "rare surprises."

46   JAMES, CLIVE. "John Berryman," The Listener
         (20 January), 87–88.
            Review of Love & Fame, noting that in that
         book, Berryman, like Corbière, presents him-
         self "in the worst possible light." The
         Dream Songs are praised and described as a
         mixture of the European tradition and contem-
         porary America, giving us a work with "per-
         sonal unhappiness as an epic subject."

47   KAMEEN, PAUL J. Review of Delusions, Etc., Best
         Sellers, XXXII (1 August), 210.
            Brief review, describing the book.

48   KANASEKI, HISAO. "Berryman no Jisatso" ["Berry-
         man's Suicide"], EigoS, CXVIII (May), 62–63.
            Discusses the difference between the mature
         detachment of such poets as Eliot and Stevens
         and the confusion of the protagonist with the
         poet in the work of Berryman and Lowell, and
         suggests that Berryman's suicide is the re-
         sult of such confusion: his suicide was a
         failure of his art.

49   KERNAN, MICHAEL. "Lines on Death and Dreams,"
         Washington Post (11 May), pp. C1–C2.

1972

(KERNAN, MICHAEL)
Description of the memorial reading given
at the Donnell Library. See also 1972.B51.

50   LASK, THOMAS. "Sought Own True Voice," New York
Times (8 January), p. 33.
Brief description of Berryman's career,
noting that the early poetry is derivative
but that Berryman found his own voice in
Homage to Mistress Bradstreet and The Dream
Songs.

51   _____. "Five Poet Friends Honor Berryman," New
York Times (11 May), p. 23.
Description of the memorial reading given
at the Donnell Library by Mark Van Doren,
Robert Fitzgerald, William Meredith, Adrienne
Rich and James Wright. See also 1972.B49.

52   LATTIMORE, RICHMOND. "Poetry Chronicle," HudR,
XXV (Autumn), 475-86 [481-82].
Review of Delusions, Etc., noting Berryman's
wit, technical ability, and the despair in the
poems.

53   LIEBERMAN, LAURENCE. "Hold the Audience!   A
Brief Memoir of John Berryman," EigoS, 118
(May), 68-70.
Memoir of Berryman's reading at the University of Illinois, describing especially Berryman's sensitivity to the troubles of others,
his own capacity for sorrow, and his kindness.
Reprinted in John Berryman Studies, I (July,
1975), 8-11 (1975.B11).

54   LINDOP, GREVEL.   Review of Love & Fame, CritQ,
XIV (Winter), 379-81 [380-81].
Love & Fame is a satirical poem based on
Berryman's experiences, tracing the notions

1972

(LINDOP, GREVEL)
of love and fame from their simplest to their
most sophisticated forms.

55 LOWELL, ROBERT. "For John Berryman," New York
Review of Books, XVIII (6 April), 3-4.
Memoir describing experiences shared with
Berryman from the forties to Berryman's death.
Berryman's early interest in wrenched syntax
and his relationships with his fellow-poets
are described, among other things.

56 McMICHAEL, JAMES. "Borges and Strand, Weak Henry,
Philip Levine," SoR, VIII (Winter), 213-24
[218-20].
Review of His Toy, His Dream, His Rest and
other volumes. Henry's "weakness" is the increasingly autobiographical aspect of The
Dream Songs. Henry is less of a character and
less interesting in the second volume than he
was in 77 Dream Songs.

57 MARTZ, LOUIS L. "Recent Poetry: Berryman and
Others," YR, LXI (Spring), 410-14.
Love & Fame is Berryman's "Last Will and
Testament"; at its center is a religious
quest.

58 MEREDITH, WILLIAM. "In Loving Memory of the Late
Author of 'The Dream Songs,'" in Richard Kelly,
John Berryman: A Checklist. Metuchen, New
Jersey: Scarecrow Press, pp. xi-xx (1972.A1).
Sensitive and informative memoir of Berry-
man at Breadloaf in 1962, visiting Frost and
putting together 77 Dream Songs, and at a
reading in Vermont in 1971, just before which
Berryman had written "The Facts & Issues."
Describes Berryman's sense of decorum, social
and literary, and his relationships with his

(MEREDITH, WILLIAM)
fellow poets. Reprinted in VQR, XLIX (Winter,
1973), 70-78 (1973.B51). Not to be confused
with this author's poem of the same title,
printed in SatR, LV (20 May, 1972), 48.

59   MILLS, RALPH J., JR. ". . . And Now a Critical
Estimate of His Unique Poetic Talents," Chicago Sun-Times Showcase (Book Week) (21 May),
p. 2.
   Review of Delusions, Etc., describing the
book, noting the language and the apparent
attraction of death, but concluding that
Berryman's "art is a triumph over suffering."

60   MURRAY, MICHELE. "Some Hint of Suicide," National
Observer (3 June), p. 21.
   Review of Delusions, Etc. It is hard to
read this "nakedly personal cry" objectively,
in light of Berryman's suicide; nevertheless,
it is clear that some of these poems rank
with the work of Donne and Hopkins.

61   NASON, RICHARD. "I Don't Think I Will Sing Any
More," Providence [Rhode Island] Journal (28
May), p. H19.
   Because of Berryman's suicide, we must
read the poems in Delusions, Etc. differently
than we would have otherwise--they take on "a
somber resonance."

62   NICOL, CHARLES. "A Poet's Book, A Poet's Death,"
Washington, D. C. Sunday Star (25 June),
p. 6C.
   Review of Delusions, Etc. Describes the
major themes of the book--religion, suicide,
art, the elegiac--and notes that perhaps the
best description of Berryman's "creed" was

1972

(NICOL, CHARLES)
  stated in the early poem, "A Point of Age":
  "We must travel in the direction of our fear."

63   NIIKURA, TOSHIKAZU. "Mask no Shi to Hadaka no
         Shi--Berryman wo megutte" ["The Poetry of the
         Mask and the Naked"], EigoS, CXVII (February),
         698-99.

64   _____. "Berryman: An Obituary," EigoS,
         CXVII (March).

65   _____. "Death's Jest Songs of Dream,"
         Chikuma (March), 4-7.

66   _____. "Berryman no Ichi" ["Berryman's
         Significance"], EigoS, CXVIII (May),
         66-67.
           Berryman's experiments in Homage to Mistress
         Bradstreet and The Dream Songs are significant
         additions to, and renewals of, the tradition
         of the modern epic started by Pound and Eliot.
         By combining the method of persona and the
         passionate rage for self-identity, Berryman
         opened a new possibility for the return of a
         modern epic of the mind. Reprinted in trans-
         lation in John Berryman Studies, I (April,
         1975), 14-18 (1975.B13).

67   NOLL, MARK. Review of Delusions, Etc., His,
         XXXIII (November), 22-23.
           Berryman is described as a Christian poet
         who at last found the "soul-satisfying City
         of God."

68   NYE, ROBERT. "Berryman--The Sequence is the
         Thing," The Times [London] (24 January),
         p. 15.

(NYE, ROBERT)
In Love & Fame, Berryman presents himself
as charming and pleasant--"a bit of a dear."
But the sequence, ending with the "Eleven
Addresses to the Lord," renders the earlier
notions of love and fame ironic.

69   PEROSA, SERGIO. "La Scomparsa di John Berryman:
      Intruzioni Finali del Poeta," Libri Nuovi,
      no. 11 (Luglio), 3.

70   PINSKY, ROBERT. "Hardy, Ransom, Berryman: A
      'Curious Air,'" Agenda, X (Spring-Summer),
      89-99.
      An examination of the curious mixture of
      Victorian elegance and colloquial "toughness"
      in the diction of the three poets points out
      the peculiarly modernistic affinities be-
      tween the three, who are all aware of the
      gulf between "the elegances of rhyme and pro-
      longed grammar" and the intolerably chaotic
      world they are describing.

71   REEVE, F. D. "On Love & Fame," Intellectual Di-
      gest, III (December), 62.
      Berryman's verse has from the beginning
      disturbed and dislocated the reader, because
      "he is who we are." In his skepticism, dis-
      illusionment and self-doubt, Berryman is the
      representative poet of the fifties and six-
      ties.

72   SAWAZAKI, JUNNOSUKE. "Berryman no Shiho Saiko"
      ["Berryman's Poetic Technique Reconsidered"],
      EigoS, CXVIII (May), 64-66.
      From the beginning of his career, Berry-
      man's poems consisted of a precarious balance
      between a rigid form and a passionate content.
      This same conflict appeared in his ambivalent

1972

(SAWAZAKI, JUNNOSUKE)
use of persona in his major work. In Berryman's last poems, there was a weakening of
that tension.

73 SKLAREW, MYRA. "Love & Fame," in Masterplots
Annual, 1972, edited by Frank N. Magill.
Englewood Cliffs, N. J.: Salem Press, pp.
201-05.
The book is a "naked" presentation of Berryman, central to which is the conflict in him
between the forces of life and death.

74 SMITH, ROBERT T. [Untitled column], Minneapolis
Tribune (9 January), p. 1B.
Memoir occasioned by Berryman's suicide,
describing Berryman's sensitivity, preoccupation with death as a subject for poetry, and
his whimsy and wit.

75 STITT, PETER A. "The Art of Poetry XVI," Paris
Review, XIV (Winter), 177-207.
Berryman's last and perhaps most important
extended interview, conducted in October of
1970. Berryman discusses his early career,
Homage to Mistress Bradstreet and the circum-
stances surrounding its composition, The
Dream Songs, his religious conversion, and
Love & Fame.

76 STRAUB, PETER. "Terror, Berryman and the New
World," Structure, I (Spring), 20-21, 25.
"The attraction toward the surreal and the
violent" in the lives and works of Berryman
and other poets in the fifties and sixties is
the result of the peculiarly American tendency
to regard "extremity as a value in itself,"
a tendency that can be traced to Poe's version
of our Romantic heritage.

77 SYMONS, JULIAN. "Another Suit," London Magazine,
     XII (December-January), 129-31.
        Berryman's religious stance in Delusions,
     Etc. is "desperately unsuccessful" and al-
     though there are some good poems in the book,
     much of it is "embarrassing."

78 TAYLOR, ROBERT. "A Poet's Anguish," Boston Globe
     (4 May), p. 45.
        In Delusions, Etc., Berryman, like Graham
     Greene, "accepts the rituals of belief yet
     is without belief." The attempts at affirma-
     tion, in view of Berryman's suicide, are not
     convincing. But despite the somber mood, "the
     originality of Berryman's quirky voice . . .
     testifies to a cancellation of chaos."

79 TOKUNAGA, SHOZO. "Shiteki na Koe, Koteki na Koe--
     Berryman to Lowell" ["Private Voice, Public
     Voice--Berryman to Lowell"], EigoS, CXVIII
     (May), 70-71.
        Berryman is essentially a lyric poet who
     produced a minor tour de force of confessional
     poetry in The Dream Songs, whereas Lowell went
     beyond his Life Studies to obtain a more
     classical, public voice in Benito Cereno and
     Prometheus Bound. Reprinted in translation
     in John Berryman Studies, I (April, 1975),
     18-23 (1975.B18).

80 VONALT, LARRY. "Berryman's Most Bright Candle,"
     Parnassus, I (Fall-Winter), 180-87.
        Essay-review of Delusions, Etc., noting
     that there are structural elements in both
     Love & Fame and Delusions, Etc. that have
     been overlooked. The structure of Love &
     Fame is "bipartite"--the first three sections
     describe Berryman on his own, the last section
     describes Berryman having accepted God.

1972

(VONALT, LARRY)
Delusions, Etc. moves from confidence in God
to doubt and back to belief.

81 WALSH, CHAD. "Poets and Their Subjects: Myth,
the GNP, the Self," Washington Post Book
World (20 February), p. 9.
In Love & Fame, Berryman quite successfully
"mangle[s] the language." The book's subjects are Berryman's ego and "its only worthy
counterfoil, God."

82 _____. "Pitfalls, Perspectives, Poetic Jus-
tice," Washington Post Book World (9 July),
p. 4
There are indications in Delusions, Etc.
that after his conversion, Berryman was moving towards a different and quieter poetic
focus, a movement ended by his suicide.

83 WEHRWEIN, AUSTIN. "Poet John Berryman Leaps to
Death," Washington Post (8 January), p. B6.
Obituary, description of Berryman's suicide,
and comments by the president of the University of Minnesota and the director of its hu-
manities program.

84 ZAND, NICHOLE. "John Berryman, Visionnaire et
Dandy," Le Monde [Paris] (8 January), p. 19.

85 ZIFF, PAUL. "A Creative Use of Language," NLH,
IV (Autumn), 107-18.
An attempt to determine what "a creative
use of language" is, and to distinguish it
from non-creative uses, concluding that it
involves creating a "melodic sound-pattern."
Some of Berryman's verse is used to exemplify
the creative use of language.

1973 A BOOKS - NONE

1973 B SHORTER WRITINGS

1   ANON. "Berryman, John," in <u>Contemporary Literary
     Criticism</u>. 2 Vols. Detroit: Gale Research.
     Vol. 1, pp. 33-34. Vol. 2, pp. 55-60.
         Selections from published criticism.

2   ANON. Review of <u>Recovery</u>, <u>Publisher's Weekly</u>,
     CCIII (29 January), 251.
         Brief discussion of the novel, noting that
     neither Severance nor the reader really come
     to terms with "the why of his disease."

3   ANON. Review of <u>Recovery</u>, <u>Kirkus Reviews</u>, XLI
     (1 February), 135.
         Brief review, noting that although the book
     is unfinished, it is the powerful record of
     "a man who was there and never came back."

4   ANON. "The Life of the Modern Poet," <u>TLS</u>, LXXII
     (23 February), 193-95.
         Essay-review of <u>Delusions, Etc</u>. describing
     in some detail Berryman's life and career,
     with useful discussions of the forms, themes
     and styles of Berryman's major works. Little
     space is devoted to <u>Delusions, Etc</u>. See
     Eileen Simpson, "Not Recommended," <u>New York
     Review of Books</u>, XX (18 October, 1973), 68
     [1973.B70] for an informed comment on the
     accuracy of this piece.

5   ANON. Review of <u>Recovery</u>, <u>NY</u>, XLIX (9 June),
     114.
         Short note, describing the book as "tedious"
     and "static."

1973

6   ANON. "Paperbacks: Nonfiction," Washington Post
     Book World (10 June), p. 13.
         Brief note describing Delusions, Etc.

7   ANON. Review of Recovery, New Republic, CLXIX
     (21 July), 27.
         Notes with sadness that the attempts at re-
     covery recounted in this book, which is "more
     a confession than a novel," did not succeed.

8   ANON. Review of Recovery, Booklist, LXX (1 Sep-
     tember), 29.
         Brief note describing the book.

9   ANON. Review of Recovery, VQR, XLIX (Autumn),
     cxxxvi.
         Brief note, describing the book as vivid
     and effective.

10   ANON. "The Sodden Soul," TLS, LXXII (30 November),
     1465.
         Jasper Stone in Recovery (the man's name is
     from a description of the heavenly city in
     Revelations) seems to represent the young
     Berryman, Severance the older one. But Berry-
     man, by eliminating Stone from the novel early
     on, avoids a possibly fruitful series of "en-
     counters between the old self and the new."
     Berryman's inability to finish the novel may
     indicate the failure of his desire to trust
     himself to divine guidance, which may be what
     drove him to suicide.

11   ANON. "Fiction," The Times [London] (6 December),
     p. 12.
         Review of Recovery and other books. The
     account of Berryman's alcoholism and the
     group therapy he undergoes is unrevised but
     still "immensely valuable and moving."

1973

12   ACKROYD, PETER. "In Flight Three Novels," Spec-
          tator, CCXXIX (1 December), 705.
          Review of Recovery and other books. By
          keeping a distance between himself and his
          protagonist, Berryman has avoided writing
          "Confessions of a Drunk," and has instead
          produced "a very fine novel."

13   ADELMAN, CLIFFORD. "A Too Brief Homage to John
          Berryman," ChiR, XIV (Spring), 124-29.
          Memoir of Berryman teaching in Providence
          in 1963, and reading in Chicago in 1964.
          Brief discussion of The Dream Songs, empha-
          sizing that the poems are "process" and that
          the choice of the dream as the framework for
          the poem is appropriate.

14   ALLEN, BRUCE. Review of Recovery, LJ, XCVIII
          (15 March), 884.
          Brief description of "this poignantly
          honest" novel.

15   ALVAREZ, A. "Dead Levelling," The Observer Re-
          view [London] (2 December), p. 35.
          Review of Recovery, describing the novel
          and noting that "as a document it is inter-
          esting, as art minimal."

16   ANGYAL, ANDREW J. "John Berryman: An Inward
          Vision," South Kent Quarterly, X (Winter),
          22-25.

17   BAUMGAERTNER, JILL. "Four Poets: Blood Type
          New," The Cresset, XXXVI (April), 16-19 [17-
          18].
          The most successful poetry in Delusions,
          Etc. is in the religious sections and in the
          poems written to artists of the past.

111

1973

18   BAYLEY, JOHN. "John Berryman: A Question of Im-
      perial Sway," Salmagundi, nos. 22-23 (Spring-
      Summer), 84-102.
          The relationship between Berryman and Henry
      in The Dream Songs is important: in The
      Dream Songs Berryman "formalizes himself."
      There is a central tension in the poem between
      the poet's words and the picture we are given
      of the poet writing those words that puts
      Henry and his actions beyond judgement. This
      is the very opposite of the European tradition
      of "getting out of your perishable tatty self"
      into a more perfect world, exemplified even by
      recent poets like Yeats and Auden. Berryman
      attempts "to discover the living ego as it has
      to be." Reprinted in Contemporary Poetry in
      America, edited by Robert Boyers. New York:
      Schocken Books, 1974 [1974.B1].

19   BELLOW, SAUL. "John Berryman, Friend," New York
      Times Book Review (27 May), pp. 1-2.
          Moving memoir of Berryman at Princeton in
      1953, in Minneapolis teaching and writing
      dream songs, giving a reading in Chicago, but
      above all, writing--drawing, until he could
      no longer, his poems "out of his very skin."
      Reprinted in Recovery, pp. ix-xix
      (1973.B20).

20   _____. "John Berryman," in Recovery. New York
      Farrar, Straus and Giroux, pp. ix-xiv.
          Reprints "John Berryman, Friend," (1973.B19).

21   BERRYHILL, MICHAEL. "Fiction," The Minnesota
      Daily [University of Minnesota] (29 May),
      pp. 12, 17.
          Review of Recovery. "The subject is the
      self" and, though Severance is not a con-
      vincing fictional character nor the book a
      convincing novel, Recovery is "an important,
      often moving fragment" of Berryman's "total
      book."

1973

22 BOARDMAN, KATHRYN G. Review of <u>Recovery</u>, St. Paul
      <u>Pioneer Press</u> (3 June), p. 12B.
         The portrait of Severance (a fictionalized
      and thus generalized Berryman) going through
      group therapy is "powerful," and reveals what
      might have been an important aspect of Berry-
      man's character--"his inability to keep out
      of other people's souls."

23 BROWNJOHN, ALAN. "Berryman Agonistes," <u>New States-</u>
      <u>man</u>, LXXXV (16 February), 238-39.
         Review of <u>Delusions, Etc.</u> and other volumes.
      The poems are very uneven, "evidence of a
      talent in disintegration," but they exhibit
      the authority of Berryman's despair.

24 BUTSCHER, EDWARD. "John Berryman: In Memorial
      Perspective," <u>GaR</u>, XXVII (Winter), 518-25.
         Survey of Berryman's work, concentrating on
      <u>The Dream Songs</u>, noting that despite its many
      faults, the poem succeeds in capturing Ameri-
      ca's "arrogant world-view and its agonies of
      secular conscience."

25 CAREY, JOHN. "Severance," <u>The Listener</u> (6 Decem-
      ber), 792-93.
         One should not take Severance, in Berryman's
      <u>Recovery</u>, simply as a projection of Berryman,
      for Berryman is doing more than writing an
      autobiographical novel--he is showing, as
      Severance's name should indicate, "the way in
      which cultural achievement and a sense of
      human values" can be separated. There are
      indications that Berryman intended to apply
      this to America as well as to his protagonist.

26 CLEMONS, WALTER. "Down the Hatch," <u>Newsweek</u>,
      LXXXI (28 May), 106-08.

1973

(CLEMONS, WALTER)
Recovery is not a successful novel, but "as
a document" of Berryman's troubles with alco-
holism, "humbles criticism."

27   ELLMANN, RICHARD AND ROBERT O'CLAIR, EDS. "John
Berryman," in The Norton Anthology of Modern
Poetry. New York: W. W. Norton, pp. 891-93.
Brief but accurate description of Berryman's
career.

28   ENGLES, JOHN. "Berryman's Last Poems," Counter-
Measures, no. 2 (1973), 177-79.
Notes the wide range of feeling in Delusions,
Etc.--from flat despair to a zany wildness
produced by "linguistic exuberance." The book
is unified by its perspective--it is "a looking
back upon life."

29   HAMILTON, IAN. "John Berryman," A Poetry Chronicle. New York: Harper and Row, pp. 111-21.
Reprints "John Berryman" (1965.B22), q. v.

30   _____. "At the End of the Line," The Observer
[London] (7 January), p. 33.
Review of Delusions, Etc. Briefly describes
Berryman's career, noting that the new style
of Berryman's late work was the result of his
realization that the style of The Dream Songs
"had become mechanical and stale." Delusions,
Etc. is "typically uneven."

31   HARRISON, KEITH. "Out There and In Here: Berryman, Ponge, and Transtromer," The Carleton
Miscellany, XIII (Spring-Summer), 111-21
[111-14].
Review of Delusions, Etc. and other books.
Describes the book, noting Berryman's roman-
ticism and his desire to be "one of the elect,"
both theologically and aesthetically.

114

32   HARSENT, DAVID. "Intimations of Mortality," Spec-
        tator (24 March), 368.
           The poems in Delusions, Etc. are weak and
        indicate that Berryman's talent had "perhaps
        begun to fail."

33   HASSAN, IHAB. "John Berryman," Contemporary
        American Literature 1945-1972: An Introduc-
        tion. New York: Frederick Ungar, pp. 99-101.
           Berryman's work was from the beginning dif-
        ficult and learned, and showed an "unappeas-
        able conscience" as Berryman faced a declining
        West. The Dream Songs "utter a fundamental
        cry of existence" and provide a new method
        for structuring the long poem.

34   _____. "John Berryman," in World Literature Since
        1945, edited by Ivan Ivask and Gero von Wil-
        pert. New York: Frederick Ungar, pp. 33-34.
           Brief description of Berryman's career,
        concentrating on the major poems and noting
        that despite the difficulty of his verse,
        Berryman "created a unique language."

35   HOWARD, JANE. "Bottle-Scarred," Time, CII (9
        July), 61ff.
           Review of Recovery. Describes the book,
        noting the insights it provides "into the
        alcoholic and suicidal character."

36   HOWES, VICTOR. "Berryman's Testament: At the
        Frontiers of Experience," Christian Science
        Monitor (6 June), p. 15.
           Review of Recovery. Although the novel is
        a fragment, it is a powerful examination of a
        man who moves to the boundaries of human ex-
        perience. It will take its place with The
        Crack-Up and The Bell Jar as a "document in
        suffering."

37 HUGHES, DANIEL. "John Berryman and the Poet's
       Passion," American Poetry Review, II (July-
       August), 19-22.
          In The Dream Songs Berryman found his voice
       through Whitman and Stephen Crane, Whitman's
       vatic self and Crane's poems which are "said
       for use." At the center of the poem are the
       notions of "Crisis" and "Lament": "Crisis"
       in the first 77 songs, "Lament" in His Toy,
       His Dream, His Rest. In Berryman's late
       poems, these notions are replaced by "Prayer."

38 JUSTUS, JAMES H. "Some Middle Generation Poetry,"
       SoR, IX (Winter), 261-68 [267-68].
          The Dream Songs is too long and "there's a
       lot of malarkey" in them, but they are an im-
       portant anatomy of our times.

39 KALSTONE, DAVID. "The Record of a Struggle With
       Prose and Life," New York Times Book Review
       (27 May), pp. 1, 3.
          At the center of Recovery is the conflict
       between Severance as a performer and the real
       Severance. That conflict was Berryman's as
       well, as evidenced by his search for a "new
       and humbling style" in the late poems.

40 KAUFFMANN, STANLEY. "Severance from Life," World,
       II (22 May), 46-47.

41 KENEDY, R. C. "John Berryman: A Study of His
       Poetry and an Appreciation, Pt. I," Art Inter-
       national, XVII (March), 75-83, 104.
          A study of The Dream Songs, concentrating
       on thematic concerns: lust, death, religion
       and especially the relationship between Berry-
       man and Henry. See also 1973.B42 and 1973.B43.

42   KENEDY, R. C. "John Berryman: An Appreciation,
        Pt. II. The Poet's Language," Art Interna-
        tional, XVII (April), 92-98.
            A discussion of the style of Berryman's
        verse, especially the syntactic oddities and
        minstrel show dialect in The Dream Songs.
        See also 1973.B41 and 1973.B43.

43   _____. "John Berryman: An Afterthought, Or,
        'The Sunset in a Cup,'" Art International,
        XVII (May), 89-96.
            A discussion of the religious sensibility
        in Berryman's verse, especially in The Dream
        Songs, and a comparison of Berryman's thought
        and poetic method with the work of other
        Twentieth Century writers, especially Pound
        and Eliot. See also 1973.B41 and 1973.B42.

44   KIRSCH, ROBERT. "A Message Put In a Bottle,"
        Los Angeles Times (7 June), p. 10D.
            Recovery is an autobiographical novel that
        transcends autobiography and moves, as Sever-
        ance struggles with himself, into the realm
        of "allegory and art."

45   LANDESS, THOMAS H. "New Urns for Old: A Look at
        Six Recent Volumes of Verse," SR, LXXXI
        (January-March), 137-57 [138-42].
            Love & Fame is "a remarkable spiritual
        memoir," a portrait of the artist. The lan-
        guage appears to be prosaic, but is more com-
        plex than that: the stylistic deviations are
        subtle and the rhetoric is "capable of almost
        any poetic task."

46   LINEBARGER, J. M. "Berryman's Sonnets: Tradition
        and the Individual Talent," CP, VI (Spring),
        19-29.

(LINEBARGER, J. M.)
Summary and explication of the <u>Sonnets</u>.
The sequence shows that in the 1940's Berryman was "a poet of two voices": the academic
voice of <u>The Dispossessed</u> and the personal
voice of the <u>Sonnets</u>, which are clearly the
precursors of <u>The Dream Songs</u>. Reprinted in
Linebarger, <u>John Berryman</u>. New York: Twayne
Publishers, 1974 (1974.A1).

47 McCABE, CHARLES. "Cornered," San Francisco
<u>Chronicle</u> (14 February), p. 43.
Brief mention of Berryman's 1971 interview
published in <u>Paris Review</u> in 1972 [1972.B75].

48 MALKOFF, KARL. "John Berryman," <u>Crowell's Hand-
book of Contemporary American Poetry</u>. New
York: Thomas Y. Crowell, pp. 25, 26, 32,
33-34, 61-67.
A useful summary and discussion of Berryman's major works from <u>The Dispossessed</u> to
<u>Delusions, Etc</u>., describing Berryman's
stylistic development and his major thematic
concerns.

49 MENDELSON, EDWARD. "How to Read Berryman's <u>Dream
Songs</u>," in <u>American Poetry Since 1960: Some
Critical Perspectives</u>, edited by Robert B.
Shaw. Cheade, Cheshire [England]: Carcanet
Press, pp. 29-43.
The "paratactic method" around which most
of the songs are organized is Husserlian--
"awareness of self, things, others," although
"often in reverse order." The poem is not
completely successful--too many of the songs
in the last half are about women and fame.
Nevertheless, when the <u>Songs</u> are successful,
"no other poem in their historical neighbor-
hood can equal them."

50   MEREDITH, WILLIAM. "Swan Songs," Poetry, CXXII
          (May), 98-103.
              In the first two books of Love & Fame,
          Berryman is "tearing up roots," attempting to
          establish a new style. Berryman is at his
          best in this volume when he is least auto-
          biographical. Despite the despairing tone of
          much of Delusions, Etc., there are some very
          happy poems in the book.

51   _____. "In Loving Memory of the Late Author of
          'The Dream Songs,'" VQR, XLIX (Winter),
          70-78.
              Reprinted from Richard Kelly, John Berryman:
          A Checklist. Metuchen, N. J.: Scarecrow
          Press, 1972. See 1972.B58.

52   MUDRICK, MARVIN. "Old Pro's With News From No-
          where," HudR, XXVI (Autumn), 545-61.
              Review of Recovery and other books. The
          implication of much of the book is that there
          can be no recovery from the alcoholic re-
          currences of the protagonist.

53   NIIKURA, TOSHIKAZU. "Berryman's Last Poems,"
          EigoS, CXIX (June).

54   NYE, ROBERT. "Poetry: Irishmen and Others," The
          Times [London] (15 February), p. 16.
              Delusions, Etc. has disturbed some critics
          because of its Christianity, which is "evan-
          gelical to the point of hysteria," but the
          book should not for that reason be avoided--
          it is often brilliant.

55   OBERG, ARTHUR. "Deer, Doors, Dark," SoR, IX
          (Winter), 243-56 [245-48].
              Love & Fame refers back to The Dream Songs,
          both by allusion and by theme, but it also

119

1973

(OBERG, ARTHUR)
looks forward to new stylistic and thematic
interests. It is an "uneven book" but the
weaknesses of the first half are balanced by
the strengths of the second.

56   PEARSON, GABRIEL. "Beyond Recovery," Manchester
[England] Guardian Weekly (15 December), p. 23.

57   PERLOFF, MARJORIE G. The Poetic Art of Robert
Lowell. Ithaca, N. Y.: Cornell University
Press, pp. xii, 174, 175-79, 182, 183.
Discussion of Berryman's "The Hell Poem,"
from Love & Fame in comparison to Lowell's
"Waking in the Blue," from Life Studies.
Berryman acts as a camera, Lowell as a parti-
cipant in the experiences he describes.

58   _____. "Poetry Chronicle: 1970-71," CL, XIV
(Winter), 97-131 [115-17].
Love & Fame is a "poetic dead end;" the
book is based on the assumption that because
Berryman is now a famous poet, the reader will
be interested in the trivialities of his life.
The language is arranged into what look like
poems, but it could just as easily have been
"a series of prose paragraphs."

59   PHILLIPS, ROBERT. "John Berryman's Literary
Offenses," The Confessional Poets. Carbon-
dale and Edwardsville: Southern Illinois
University Press, pp. 92-106.
In The Dream Songs, Berryman achieved some
brilliant verse by speaking through the mask
of Henry. But when, in Love & Fame, "Berryman dropped the third person, that which had
been latently bad in his work became out-
rageously so." Love & Fame suffers from
triviality, too much ego-involvement, bad

(PHILLIPS, ROBERT)
puns, lack of memorable·images and syntactic
difficulties. Delusions, Etc. is quieter and
more humble, and "redeems his reputation,
tarnished so badly by the offenses of Love &
Fame." Reprints and slightly expands "Balling
the Muse," North American Review, CCLVII (Winter, 1971-72) (1971.B24).

60   PORTERFIELD, JO. "Berryman's 'A Strut for
Roethke,'" Expl, XXXII (December), item 25.
'Strut' is the term for the return from the
cemetery in a New Orleans funeral. The poem
moves from grief to comfort in the fact that
Roethke has reached stasis and need try no
longer "to order the world with words."

61   _____. "The Melding of a Man: Berryman, Henry
and the Ornery Mr. Bones," SWR, LVIII
(Winter), 30-46.
In The Dream Songs, Henry progresses from
the cage of guilt, anxiety and "separateness
from the world," created by his father's
suicide, to an ability to "reach out beyond
himself" through his poetry, his love for his
wife and his children. He is still in a
"middle ground" at the end of the poem, but
he has discovered the saving value of the
"old verities of the heart."

62   PRITCHARD, WILLIAM. "Metaphysical Hangover,"
New Statesman, LXXXVI (30 November), 826.
Review of Recovery. Except for some of
The Dream Songs, this is Berryman's "most
honest and most imaginative performance."

63   RICKS, CHRISTOPHER. "Walking the Line," The Sunday Times [London] (7 January), p. 30.

1973

(RICKS, CHRISTOPHER)
Review of <u>Delusions, Etc</u>. Points out
Berryman's obsession with delusion in the
<u>Paris Review</u> interview and notes that Berry-
man's religious conversion did not produce
good religious poetry: "it is cruelly sad"
that Berryman "should have shuddered to a
halt" with this verse, the forerunner of which
is not the poetry of Hopkins but of Francis
Thompson.

64 RODMAN, SELDEN. "Petrified by Gorgon Egos," <u>New
Leader</u>, LVI (22 January), 20-21.
Review of <u>Delusions, Etc</u>. and other volumes.
Berryman's work has been "overpraised." His
ego is so large that in this volume about his
conversion, "God comes out second best."

65 RUDNICK, MICHAEL. "<u>Delusions, Etc</u>. of John Berryman," <u>Masterplots Annual, 1973</u>, edited by
Frank N. Magill. Englewood Cliffs, N. J.:
Salem Press, pp. 108-11.
Description of the book, noting that the
religious poems are less peaceful than those
in <u>Love & Fame</u>. Berryman's attitude is "per-
vasively uncertain."

66 RYAN, F. L. Review of <u>Recovery</u>, <u>Best Sellers</u>,
XXXIII (1 July), 150.
Brief note, describing the book.

67 SCHORER, MARK. "The Lonely Calm," <u>Atlantic</u>,
CCXXXII (August), 92-94.
Review of <u>Recovery</u>. In creating Severance
and Jasper Stone, Berryman splits himself into two voices, just as he had done in <u>Homage
to Mistress Bradstreet</u> and <u>The Dream Songs</u>,
in order to objectify and more easily handle
his desperation.

68   SERGEANT, HOWARD. "Poetry Review," English, XXII
         (Autumn), 121-24 [123].
             Brief review of Delusions, Etc., noting that
         it is the work of a man "driven beyond the
         limits of human endurance."

69   SEYMOUR-SMITH, MARTIN. "John Berryman," Funk and
         Wagnalls' Guide to World Literature. New
         York: Funk and Wagnalls, pp. 162-63.
             Brief discussion of Berryman's career with
         emphasis placed on The Dream Songs. Although
         we do not know what effect the poem will have
         after years of critical attention, "its im-
         portance is unquestioned."

70   SIMPSON, EILEEN [BERRYMAN]. "Not Recommended,"
         New York Review of Books, XX (18 October), 68.
             Letter from Berryman's first wife which
         notes with dismay that in his article, "Last
         Testament" [1973.B81], John Thompson recom-
         mended "The Life of the Modern Poet" [1973.B4],
         for that article is filled with biographical
         and interpretive errors.

71   STEFANIK, ERNEST C. "A Cursing Glory: John
         Berryman's Love & Fame," Renascence, XXV
         (Summer), 115-27.
             Reading Love & Fame simply as a collection
         of lyrics and refusing to consider the poems
         on their own terms have led critics to a mis-
         understanding of the work. It is a narrative
         that takes the form of a religious quest,
         moving from youthful excesses to a discovery
         of God's love.

72   _____. "Bibliography: John Berryman Criticism,"
         WCR, VIII (October), 45-52.
             A list of 366 items about Berryman divided
         into the following categories: Interviews,

1973

(STEFANIK, ERNEST C.)
    Bibliographies, Biography, Homage, and
    Criticism (including book reviews).

73 STITT, PETER. "Berryman's Last Poems," CP, VI
        (Spring), 5-12.
        Brief and accurate description of Berry-
    man's work up to Delusions, Etc., which is
    discussed in detail. The book's intent is
    described in one of the epigraphs: "L'art
    est religieux." The religious feeling in the
    book, however, is ambiguous, containing both
    certainty and doubt.

74 _____. "John Berryman: Poetry and Personality,"
        Ann Arbor Review, no. 17 (1973), 92-95.
        92-95.
        Review of Recovery. Points out the tension
    in all of Berryman's work between the formal,
    technical aspects of poetry and Berryman's
    own "incredibly strong personality." Briefly
    traces the course of this tension in Berry-
    man's work from the early poems to Recovery,
    which is almost all personality and not a
    work of art.

75 STRAND, MARK. "Landscape and the Poetry of Self,"
        Prose, VI (Spring), 169-83.

76 SUPPAN, STEVEN. "Tales of an Editor," Minnesota
        Daily [University of Minnesota] (8 October),
        p. 11.
        Interview with Berryman's editor, Robert
    Giroux, on the occasion of his speaking at
    the University of Minnesota. Giroux describes
    his relationship with Berryman from their
    friendship at Columbia through the publication
    of Homage to Mistress Bradstreet and Berryman's
    subsequent work.

124

77   SYMONS, JULIAN. "Taking Off," The Sunday Times
        [London] (25 November), p. 40.
        Review of Recovery and other volumes.
        Brief note, describing the book as "painful
        and disappointing."

78   TAYLOR, MARK. Review of Recovery, Commonweal,
        XCIX (28 December), 349-51.
        Notes many of the correspondences between
        Severance's plight and America's plight,
        speculating that Berryman was going to use
        alcoholism "as a metaphor for the more gener-
        alized malaise" of the country.

79   TEMPLE, JOANNE. Review of Recovery, The Village
        Voice (8 November), pp. 34-36.

80   THOMES, A. BOYD. "Berryman . . . The Price He
        Paid For His Poetry," Minneapolis Tribune
        (8 July), 8D-9D.
        Review of Delusions, Etc. and brief memoir
        of Berryman during the period of the writing
        of The Dream Songs. The author was a close
        friend of Berryman's and his physician. De-
        scribes Berryman as writing out of his own
        emotional chaos. Also describes Berryman's
        worsening alcoholism, which led to the experi-
        ences recounted in Recovery.

81   THOMPSON, JOHN. "Last Testament," New York Review
        of Books, XX (9 August), 3-4, 6.
        Essay-review of Recovery, describing Berry-
        man's life and his accomplishments. Notes
        that Recovery might have been made into "a
        distinguished novel" if Berryman had finished
        it. See 1973.B70 for a note on the accuracy
        of Thompson's major source.

1973

82   TULIP, JAMES. "The 'Tough Songs' of John Berryman," SoRA, VI (September), 257-68.

83   VAN DOREN, MARK. "John Berryman: 1914-1972," Proceedings of the American Academy of Arts and Letters and the National Institute of Arts and Letters. New York: American Academy of Arts and Letters, pp. 101-03.
      Brief memoir of Berryman, description of his personal qualities and his achievements, and a quotation from a letter to Van Doren from Berryman evaluating himself and his work.

84   VENDLER, HELEN. "Poetry: Ammons, Berryman, Cummings," YR, LXII (Spring), 412-25 [424-25].
      Review of Delusions, Etc. and other books. Berryman's religious poems are "no good." It is too much to have expected Berryman to invent a "convincing new stance" and style to match his religious conversion.

85   WINTERS, YVOR. "Three Poets," in Yvor Winters: Uncollected Essays and Reviews, edited by Francis Murphy. Chicago: Swallow Press, pp. 169-71.
      Reprinted from HudR, I (Autumn, 1948), 404-05 (1948.B19), q. v.

1974 A BOOKS

1   LINEBARGER, J. M. John Berryman. New York: Twayne Publishers.
      The first published full-length examination of Berryman's poetry, a chronological study,

(LINEBARGER, J. M.)
tracing major themes and the development of
Berryman's style from "Twenty Poems" to
Delusions, Etc. Berryman began, under the
influence of Yeats and Auden, as an Academic
poet, technically proficient but without a
voice of his own. Berryman's development from
this point on was the result of his willingness
to take risks--"risks with style and with his
own psyche." Berryman's Sonnets are the result of his taking the first of those risks;
in them Berryman solved the problem of writing
personal poetry that was at the same time universal. In Homage to Mistress Bradstreet,
Berryman risked only his style; he did not
allow his own self into the poem. For this
reason, the poem is "the dead-end of purely
Academic" poetry for Berryman. It gave him a
stanza form but little else. In The Dream
Songs, Berryman brought together the elements
he had experimented with in his earlier verse,
and wrote a poem that combined the best of
both Academic and Beat poetry.

2   STEFANIK, ERNEST C. John Berryman: A Descriptive
Bibliography. Pittsburgh Series in Bibliogra-
phy. Pittsburgh: University of Pittsburgh
Press.
Describes books, pamphlets and keepsakes by
Berryman published in the U. S. and Great
Britain, arranged into the following cate-
gories: Separate Publications, First-Appear-
ance Contributions to Books, Contributions to
Periodicals, Collected Materials Reprinted in
Anthologies, Interviews, Phonorecordings,
Dust-Jacket Blurbs, Poetry Selections by
Berryman. There are two appendices, "A Chro-
nology of the Publications of Works by Berry-
man" and "Periodicals in Which Material by

(STEFANIK, ERNEST C.)
Berryman First Appeared." There are many
notes, listing variants in poems that Berryman revised and detailing the circumstances
surrounding the publication of certain works.
No works about Berryman are included.

1974 B   SHORTER WRITINGS

1   BAYLEY, JOHN. "On John Berryman," in Contemporary
Poetry in America, edited by Robert Boyers.
New York: Schocken Books.
Reprints "John Berryman: A Question of
Imperial Sway," Salmagundi, nos. 22-23
(Spring-Summer, 1973), 84-102 [1973.B18], q. v.

2   BROWNE, MICHAEL DENNIS. "Henry Fermenting: Debts
to The Dream Songs," OhR, XV (Winter), 75-87.
A discussion, partially based on letters
from younger poets, of the possible areas of
influence of The Dream Songs: the use of the
persona, the mixture of traditional poetic
diction and colloquial language; and "the
massive theme" of the death of the father.

2a CLOSE, ROY M. "Schorer Sees Berryman Key in Unfinished Book," Minneapolis Star (9 May),
p. 6D.

3   DUNN, DOUGLAS. "Gaiety and Lamentation: The Defeat of John Berryman," Encounter, XLIII
(August), 72-77.
Discussion of Berryman's career, concentrating on The Dream Songs.   Behind the eccen-
tricities of style and the sometimes overly-
personal references in The Dream Songs lies
Berryman's essential humanity, honestly
anguished "at the cruelty of the world."   His
"defeat" is the defeat of the alienated poet:

(DUNN, DOUGLAS)
those who read his work remain unaffected by
it; their response is limited to literary
cliches.

4   EWART, GAVIN. "The Horse's Mouth," Ambit, no.
57 (1974), 43-44.
Recovery is painful to read, not only because we know that Berryman did not succeed
at his own attempt to recover, but also because the portrait of therapy and institu-
tional life is movingly described. The book
could have been written by many other people,
perhaps, but not "half as well."

5   HAYES, ANN. Review of Delusions, Etc., Three
Rivers Poetry Journal, nos. 3-4 (Spring),
62-63.
Reprinted in an expanded version as
"Delusions, Etc. and the Art of Distance,"
John Berryman Studies, I (January, 1975)
[1975.B6], q. v.

6   HEYEN, WILLIAM. "John Berryman: A Memoir and an
Interview," OhR, XV (Winter), 46-65.
Memoir of Berryman's reading at SUNY at
Brockport, describing, with affection and
sensitivity, Berryman's actions, appearance
and emotional states as well as the whirl-
wind effect of his two-day visit. The interview is a transcription of a television interview conducted on that occasion. Berryman discusses, among other things, his early
career, the Sonnets, and the circumstances
surrounding the writing of parts of Homage
to Mistress Bradstreet.

7   McCLATCHY, J. D. "Blood-Hot and Personal: The
Tradition of Contemporary Confessional Poetry."

JOHN BERRYMAN: A REFERENCE GUIDE

     Ph.D. dissertation, Yale-University.
     Berryman is one of four confessional poets
     discussed.

8   MONTAGUE, JOHN. "Memoir of an American Poet in
     Dublin," _Hibernia_ (24 May).

9   NEILL, EDWARD. "Ambivalence of Berryman: An
     Interim Report," _CritQ_, XVI (Autumn), 267-76.
       Discussion of Berryman's work, especially
     Love & Fame, noting Berryman's "shocking
     honesty," and emphasizing that Berryman as a
     poet stands not for health but for the moral
     chaos of our culture.

10   PLOTKIN, FREDERICK. "Fiction," _Britannica Book
     of the Year, 1974_. Chicago: Encyclopedia
     Britannica, p. 426.
       Brief note on _Recovery_.

11   SIMPSON, LOUIS. "On Berryman's _Recovery_," _OhR_,
     XV (Winter), 112-14.
       Berryman and a whole generation of "con-
     fessional poets" went wrong by being inter-
     ested only in fame. In _Recovery_, Berryman is
     merely "pleading to be liked," and the book
     is "unreadable."

12   STAUFFER, DONALD BARLOW. _A Short History of
     American Poetry_. New York: E. P. Dutton,
     pp. 377-82.
       Description of Berryman's career, concen-
     trating on his attempt to forge a style of
     his own, and noting the continual "painful
     intellectual awareness" of his verse from the
     beginning.

13   STEFANIK, ERNEST C.   "A John Berryman Checklist,"
        BB, XXXI (January-March), 1-4, 28.
            A checklist of 172 items listing Berryman's
        writings in the following major categories:
        Separate Publications (poetry, prose, fic-
        tion); Contributions to Books (poetry, prose);
        Contributions to Periodicals (poetry, prose,
        fiction). See also 1975.A3.

14   STITT, PETER.   "John Berryman: The Dispossessed
        Poet," OhR, XV (Winter), 66-74.
            Berryman, like other modern poets, was dis-
        possessed by his society, which pays no
        attention to poets, and possessed by inner
        demons which he tried to exorcise by turning
        unsuccessfully to the community of poets,
        love, and, in his last work, religion. Berry-
        man's "body of work leads us inexorably and
        inevitably to the point of suicide."

15   THOMPSON, SUSAN.   "Boundaries of the Self: Poetry
        by Frost, Roethke and Berryman, Considered in
        the Light of the Language of Schizophrenia."
        Ph.D. dissertation, University of Texas
        (Austin).
            77 Dream Songs is the Berryman work examined.
        Berryman "concentrates on the contradictions
        in his identity," and paradoxically, while
        revealing himself also hides himself through
        the use of allusions, syntactic obscurity and
        association.

1975 A   BOOKS - NONE

1975 B   SHORTER WRITINGS

1   ANON.   "Berryman, John."   The New Encyclopedia
        Britannica: Micropaedia.   V. 1.   Chicago:

1975

(ANON.)
Encyclopedia Britannica, p. 1017.
    Brief discussion of Berryman's career.

2   ALBERTI, A. J.   "Henry on His Mind," Moons and
    Lion Tailes, I (Spring), 29-42.
        Discussion of The Dream Songs, concentrating
    on the relationship between Berryman and Hen-
    ry, the "triadic structure" of the individual
    songs and the language of the poem.

3   ARPIN, GARY Q.   "'I Am Their Musick': Lamenta-
    tions and The Dream Songs," John Berryman
    Studies, I (January), 1-6.
        Notes the resemblances between Lamentations
    and The Dream Songs, discovering in Lamenta-
    tions the source of some of Berryman's imagery
    and noting that the references to Lamentations
    "serve to indicate the relationship between
    the poet and his world and the poet and his
    audience."

4   _____.   "Mistress Bradstreet's Discontents,"
    John Berryman Studies, I (July), 2-7.
        Analysis of the poem, concentrating on the
    conflict between the instinctual needs of its
    protagonists and their commitments to their
    cultures.

5   HAFFENDEN, JOHN.   "Berryman's 'Certainty Before
    Lunch,'" John Berryman Studies, I (July),
    15-16.
        Analysis of the poem, locating the source of
    Berryman's scientific information and describ-
    ing the irony that is at the center of the
    poem: Berryman "inverts the common assump-
    tion that science can attain more certainty
    of its subject than can theology."

6   HAYES, ANN. "Delusions, Etc. and the Art of Dis-
       tance," John Berryman Studies, I (January),
       6-10.
         Berryman attempts to avoid the inherent
       danger in confessional poetry of embarrass-
       ment and self-absorption in several ways: by
       accepting the formal structure of canonical
       hours; by using the voice of Henry; by taking
       a flatly honest self-view; by addressing
       others.

7   _____. "The Voices of John Berryman," John
       Berryman Studies, I (July), 17-20.
       Reprinted from the International Poetry
       Forum, 1970 [1970.B15], q. v.

8   HEYEN, WILLIAM. "Delusion and Her Daughters:
       John Berryman's Recovery," SoR, XI (Summer),
       721-24.
        Description of the novel, concentrating on
       the enormously difficult and finally unsuc-
       cessful attempt at recovery that the book re-
       counts.

9   KELLY, RICHARD J. AND ERNEST STEFANIK. "John
       Berryman: A Supplemental Checklist," John
       Berryman Studies, I (April), 25-35.
        A checklist of secondary materials, supple-
       menting Richard Kelly, John Berryman: A Check-
       list [1972.A1]. Includes reviews of Berry-
       man's works and general critical and biograph-
       ical works.

10   _____. "John Berryman: A Supplemental Check-
       list. Part II," John Berryman Studies, I
       (July), 23-31.
        Continuation of 1975.B9. Includes general
       critical and biographical works.

1975

11   LIEBERMAN, LAURENCE. "Hold the Audience! A
     Brief Memoir of John Berryman," John Berryman
     Studies, I (July), 8-11.
        Reprinted from EigoS, CXVIII (May, 1972),
     68-70 [1972.B53], q. v.

12   LINEBARGER, J. M. "A Commentary on Berryman's
     Sonnets," John Berryman Studies, I (January),
     13-24.
        Poem-by-poem commentary, explaining the
     sonnets and identifying literary and histori-
     cal allusions.

13   NIIKURA, TOSHIKAZU. "Berryman's Significance,"
     John Berryman Studies, I (April), 14-18.
        Reprints in translation, "Berryman no Ichi,"
     EigoS, CXVIII (May, 1972), 66-67 [1972.B66],
     q. v.

14   OBERG, ARTHUR. "John Berryman: Prosody and
     Overneeds," John Berryman Studies, I (January),
     24-27.
        In reading and judging The Dream Songs, we
     must think of prosody in larger terms than
     simply meter and scansion, for in Berryman's
     poem, as in much Twentieth Century poetry,
     there is a great deal of overstressing and
     understressing, and the poem on the page may
     be very different from the poem "meant to be
     read aloud."

15   PAVLOVCAK, MICHAEL. "The Method of The Dream
     Songs," John Berryman Studies, I (January),
     27-29.
        Discussion of The Dream Songs in light of
     the epigraph to 77 Dream Songs from Olive
     Schreiner: "But there is another method."
     Examines the quote in its context, and notes
     that, applied to The Dream Songs, it "results
     in an open-ended literary work."

1975

16   STANFORD, ANN.   "The Elegy of Mourning in Modern
        American and English Poetry," SoR, XI
        (Spring), 357-72.
            One of the elegies examined in detail is
        Berryman's "Formal Elegy." "Lycidas" was
        Berryman's model; the poem is "a full elegy"
        in the pastoral tradition.

17   STITT, PETER.   "'Bitter Sister, Victim! I Miss
        You': John Berryman's Homage to Mistress
        Bradstreet," John Berryman Studies, I (April),
        2-11.
            Analysis of the poem, concentrating on Anne
        Bradstreet's physical environment and meta-
        physical attitudes, and the relations between
        her and the poet.

18   TOKUNAGA, SHOZO.   "Private Voice, Public Voice--
        John Berryman and Robert Lowell," John Berry-
        man Studies, I (April), 18-23.
            Reprints in translation, "Shiteki na Koe,
        Koteki na Koe," EigoS, CXVIII (May, 1972),
        70-71 [1972.B79], q. v.

135

Index

The following index includes, arranged alphabetically in one sequence, the authors and titles of all works listed in this bibliography, as well as the subjects of those works--Berryman's books, and in those cases in which specific short poems are discussed in detail in an article, those poems (identified by a "B" in parenthesis following the title). It has not been possible, of course, to list every short poem discussed in longer works.

The index also includes a number of specialized subject headings, under the main heading of "Berryman, John": appointments, awards and honors; bibliographies; biography; interviews with; memoirs of. The subheading "biography" contains references not only to books and articles describing Berryman's life, but also to newspaper and magazine announcements of events in his life not covered by the other subheadings. I have shortened some titles where it was necessary and would not be confusing.

Index references are not to page numbers, but to item numbers. To find a specific item, turn to the date, section and number listed.

INDEX

"Berryman--The Sequence is
the Thing," 1972.B68
"Berryman Wins $1,000 for
Poetry," 1969.B52
"Berryman: Without Impu-
dence and Vanity,"
1969.B26
"Berryman's 'A Strut for
Roethke,'" 1973.B60
"Berryman's Achievement,"
1969.B30
"Berryman's 'Certainty Be-
fore Lunch,'" 1975.B5
"Berryman's Chaplinesque,"
1965.B24
"Berryman's Dream Songs,"
1965.B33
"Berryman's Dream Songs
Combine Comic and
Terrifying," 1964.B16
"Berryman's Dream World,"
1969.B38
"Berryman's Dreams of
Death," 1968.B39
"Berryman's Everyman,"
1969.B43
"Berryman's Last Poems,"
1973.B28,B53,B73
"Berryman's Last Poems Re-
flect His Relationship
with Subjects,"
1972.B34
"Berryman's Long Dream,"
1969.B21
"Berryman's Most Bright
Candle," 1972.B80
"Berryman's Nunc Dimittis,"
1969.B9
"Berryman's Poems Span 40
Years," 1967.B13
"Berryman's 77 Dream Songs,"
1971.B23

"Berryman's Significance,"
1975.B13
"Berryman's Songs," 1965.B37
"Berryman's Sonnets,"
1968.B38
Berryman's Sonnets,
1967.B2-B5,B11,B14-
B15,B19-B22,B24,B29,
B30-B34; 1968.B7-B8,
B10-B11,B13,B17-B18,
B21-B22,B28,B30,B33,
B35,B38,B40,B42,B44;
1969.A1,B31,B39,B51;
1970.B7,B15,B17-B18;
1971.A1; 1973.B46,B48;
1974.A2; 1975.B12
"Berryman's Sonnets: Tra-
dition and the Indi-
vidual Talent,"
1973.B46
"Berryman's Testament,"
1973.B36
"Berryman's The Dream
Songs," 1971.B29
"Berryman's Vein Profound,"
1967.B31
Bewley, Marius, 1967.B11
"Beyond Recovery," 1973.B56
"Bibliography: John Berry-
man Criticism,"
1973.B72
The Bit Between My Teeth,
1965.B39
"'Bitter Sister, Victim!'"
1975.B17
Blackmur, R. P., 1941.B3
Bland, Peter, 1968.B10
"Blood-Hot and Personal,"
1974.B7
Blum, Morgan, 1951.B9
Bly, Robert, 1970.B6

"The City and the House,"
1970.B16
Clark, Virginia Prescott,
1968.A1
Clarke, Austin, 1959.B4
Clarke, Clorinda, 1951.B12
Clemons, Walter, 1972.B32;
1973.B26
Close, Roy M., 1972.B33-
B34; 1974.B2a
"The Cold Heart, the Cold
City," 1949.B1
"Colonel Shaw in American
Poetry," 1972.B20
"A Commentary on Berryman's
Sonnets," 1975.B12
"Confidences," 1972.B22
"Congested Funeral,"
1969.B6
Connelly, Kenneth, 1969.B15
Conrad, Sherman, 1941.B4
"Constellation of Five
Young Poets," 1941.B9
"A Contrast of Excellence,"
1957.B14
"Conversation With Berry-
man," 1970.B19
Cook, Bruce, 1972.B35
Cooper, Philip, 1970.B9
Corke, Hilary, 1959.B5
"Cornered," 1973.B47
"Correspondence: The
Staging of King Lear,"
1946.B1
Corrigan, Robert A.,
1969.B16
Cott, Jonathan, 1964.B9;
1965.B15
"The Couch and Poetic In-
sight," 1965.B31
Cournos, John, 1951.B13

Courtney, Winifred F.,
1968.B14
Creation's Very Self,
1969.B40
"A Creative Use of Language,"
1972.B85
"Critical Biography of
Stephen Crane,"
1951.B19
Curley, Dorothy Nyren,
1969.B17
Curran, Mary Doyle,
1965.B16
"Current Books of Poetry,"
1972.B29
"A Cursing Glory," 1973.B71
Cushman, Jerome, 1967.B12;
1968.B15; 1970.B10

Daiches, David, 1948.B6
Dale, Peter, 1971.B8;
1972.B36
Daniel, Robert, 1941.B5
Davis, Douglas M., 1969.B18
Davis, Robert Gorham,
1950.B5
Davison, Peter, 1965.B17
Day, Stacey B., 1972.B37
"Dead Levelling," 1973.B15
"The Death of John Berry-
man," 1972.B44
"Death Was a Recurring
Theme in Life Work of
Poet Berryman,"
1972.B33
"Death's Jest Songs of
Dream," 1972.B65
"Declining Occasions,"
1968.B13
"Deep in the Unfriendly
City," 1948.B10

Harsent, David, 1972.B42; 1973.B32
Hart, H. W., 1950.B6
Hart, James D., 1965.B23
Hartgen, Stephen, 1972.B43
Hassan, Ihab, 1973.B33,B34
"Hats Off--A Genius," 1969.B44
Havighurst, Walter, 1951.B15
Hayes, Ann, 1970.B15; 1974.B5; 1975.B6,B7
Hayman, Ronald, 1970.B16
Hazo, Samuel, 1972.B44
"He Left a Note," 1971.B16
"The Hell Poem" (B), 1973.B57
"Henry Fermenting," 1974.B2
"Henry Himself," 1969.B13
"Henry on His Mind," 1975.B2
"Henry Pussycat, He Come Home Good," 1969.B15
"Henry's Hobble," 1969.B20
"Henry's Youth," 1968.B44
"Henry Tasting All the Secret Bits of Life," 1965.B27
"Hero and Victim" 1951.B25
Herzberg, Max J., 1962.B2
Heyen, William, 1970.B17; 1974.B6; 1975.B8
Hicks, Granville, 1952.B3
His Thoughts Made Pockets and the Plane Buckt, 1959.B11; 1961.B1; 1974.A1
"His Toy, His Dream, His Rest," 1969.B53

His Toy, His Dream, His Rest (See also The Dream Songs), 1968.B3-B4,B6,B9,B15,B20,B23-B24,B26,B29,B37,B39, B45,B47; 1969.B4,B6-B11,B13-B15,B19-B20, B23,B26-B27,B29-B30, B35,B38,B49,B50,B53, B56; 1970.B12,B16, B22; 1971.B10,B27; 1972.B56
Hoffman, Daniel, 1970.B18
Holder, Alan, 1969.B28
"Hold the Audience!" 1972.B53; 1975.B11
Hollis, C. Carroll, 1951.B16
Holmes, John, 1940.B1; 1956.B2
Holmes, Richard, 1969.B29
"Homage in Measure to Mr. Berryman," 1958.B1
"Homage to Berryman's Homage," 1969.B25
"Homage to Mistress Brad-street," 1957.B15
Homage to Mistress Brad-street (See also Homage to Mistress Bradstreet and Other Poems), 1956.B1-B7; 1957.B3,B5-B8, B10-B17; 1960.B2; 1964.B14; 1966.B6,B9; 1967.B20, B25; 1968.A1,B18,B43; 1969.A1,B25,B28,B46; 1970.B13,B15,B18,B23; 1971.A1; 1972.B66,B75; 1973.B4,B48; 1974.A1; 1975.B4,B17

INDEX